BUSINESS PRACTICE 2 | Curriculum Map

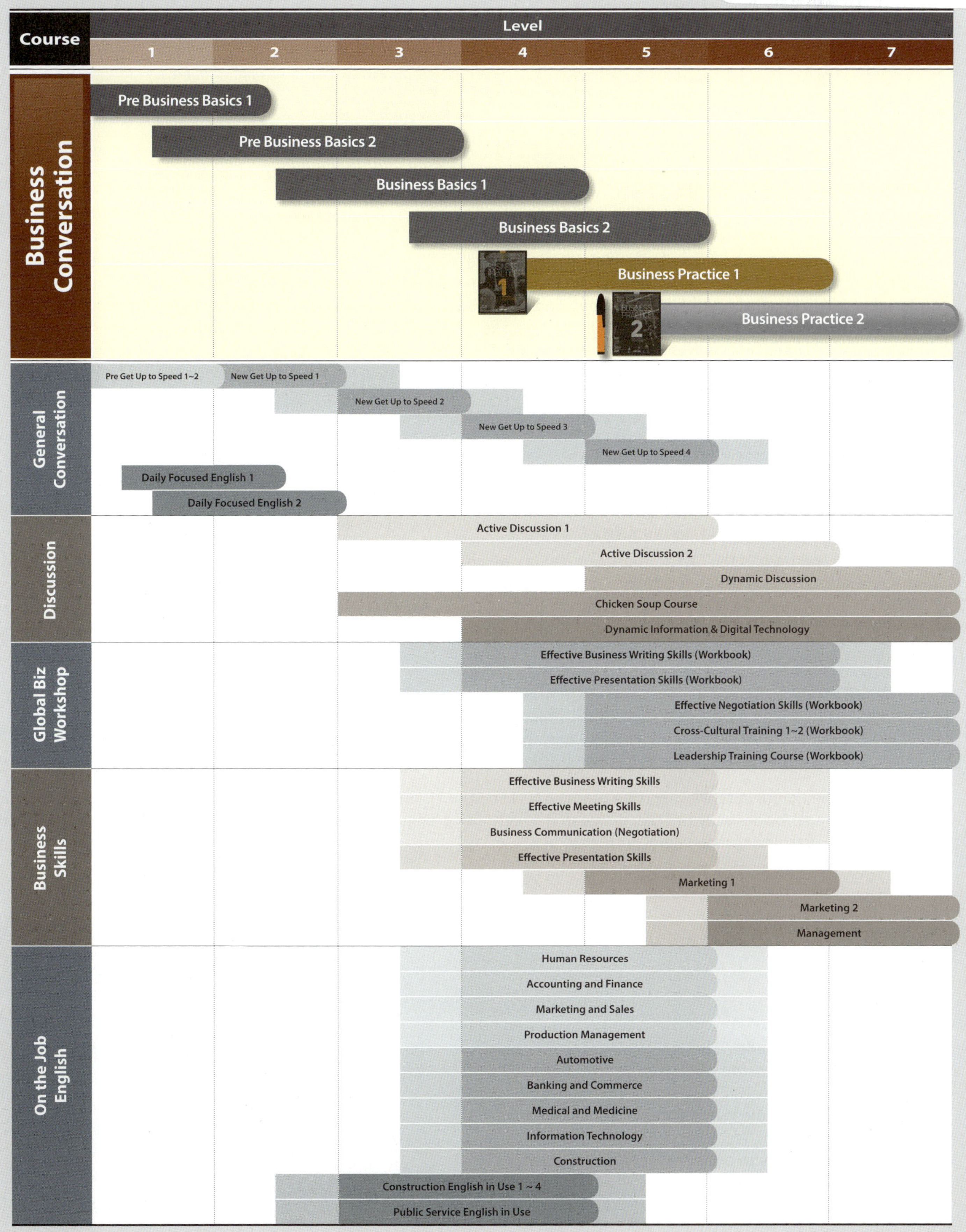

Course	Level 1	2	3	4	5	6	7
Business Conversation	Pre Business Basics 1	Pre Business Basics 2	Business Basics 1	Business Basics 2	Business Practice 1	Business Practice 1	Business Practice 2
					Business Practice 2		
General Conversation	Pre Get Up to Speed 1~2	New Get Up to Speed 1	New Get Up to Speed 2	New Get Up to Speed 3	New Get Up to Speed 4		
	Daily Focused English 1	Daily Focused English 2					
Discussion				Active Discussion 1	Active Discussion 2	Dynamic Discussion	
				Chicken Soup Course			
				Dynamic Information & Digital Technology			
Global Biz Workshop				Effective Business Writing Skills (Workbook)			
				Effective Presentation Skills (Workbook)			
					Effective Negotiation Skills (Workbook)		
					Cross-Cultural Training 1~2 (Workbook)		
					Leadership Training Course (Workbook)		
Business Skills				Effective Business Writing Skills			
				Effective Meeting Skills			
				Business Communication (Negotiation)			
				Effective Presentation Skills			
					Marketing 1		
						Marketing 2	
						Management	
On the Job English				Human Resources			
				Accounting and Finance			
				Marketing and Sales			
				Production Management			
				Automotive			
				Banking and Commerce			
				Medical and Medicine			
				Information Technology			
				Construction			
		Construction English in Use 1 ~ 4					
		Public Service English in Use					

Business Practice 2

Introduction

Carrot House Methodology

Andragogical Approach & Productive English

The teaching of children (pedagogy) and adult learning (andragogy) are distinctively different. Pedagogy is akin to training and encourages convergent thinking and rote learning. It is compulsory, centered on the teacher and the imparting of information with minimal control by the learner. Andragogy, by contrast, is about education as freedom. It encourages divergent thinking and active learning. It is voluntary, learner oriented and opens up vistas for continuing learning. Adults need to feel independent and in control of their learning. Therefore, Carrot House curriculum is based on andragogy and is designed to encourage learners' participation and engagement by providing more task-based activities and opportunities to frequently interact in the classroom.

People want to achieve communicative competence when they learn other languages. English education in EFL environments has been rather focused on the receptive skills of English—listening and reading—which simply increases learners' knowledge about a language, not the competence of using it. If people are well equipped with productive skills—speaking and writing—they will be competent in English communication.

This is why Carrot House curriculum is designed to enhance learners' productive skills throughout the course. This andragogical approach of the Carrot House Curriculum, which focuses on productive English, will enable learners to achieve communication skills necessary for global competence. Carrot House's teaching philosophy and curriculum combine to provide a "Language for Success" for all learners.

Communicative Language Learning (CLL)

This communicative interaction, the essential component of language acquisition, does not occur in a typical, non-meaningful, fun-oriented conversation with native speakers. It occurs in a negotiated interaction through which a well-trained teacher provides the comprehensible input that is appropriate to the learners. The learners, at the same time, actively utilize the opportunities given to them by the teachers.

To this end, the Communicative Language Learning (CLL) method is employed in the field of Foreign Language Acquisition. The CLL method provides activities that are geared toward using language pragmatically, authentically and functionally with the intention of achieving meaningful purposes.

Course Overview

I. Objectives

BUSINESS PRACTICE series is designed to enhance learners' communication skills in the workplace by providing a wide range of situations involved in business. Each series is targeted at intermediate level learners. Through constant classroom interactions, learners can improve their productive proficiency to achieve success in international transactional situations.

II. How to Use Business Practice 2

The book consists of 16 lessons based on topics of great interest to everyone involved in international business. The composition of each lesson is as below.

Learning Objectives
Set clear goals to acknowledge target learning of each lesson.
- Go over the learning objectives with learners to understand the learning focus.
- Review the objectives at the end of each lesson to reinforce each point.

Warm Up Activities
Stimulate learners' thinking and put them at ease in an English speaking environment by asking the topic-related questions provided.
- Pair up the class and encourage the pairs to talk about their experience related to the questions.
- Give them opportunities to share the contents of their discussions with the whole class.
- Encourage learners to deliver short speeches as a warm up activity.

Fill in the blanks with the correct words
Check out the key vocabulary to better understand the situation presented in the following dialogue.
- Ask learners to read the meanings of some vocabulary and fill in the blanks with the correct words.
- Ensure they understand the meanings of all the words they do not know.

Dialogue
Role play the dialogue to practice English speaking in various situations native business people would face on a daily basis at work. Help learners improve their comprehension skills and acquire useful expressions.
- Pair up the class and practice the dialogue (role play).
- Give feedback on each learner's role play.
- There are two activities which are connected to the dialogue as below:
  A. Situation - Review by having learners summarize the situation in their own words.
  B. Questions - Encourage students to discuss the topic more in depth by providing discussion questions.

Business Practice 2

Language Practice
Reinforce useful chunks in dialogues through meaningful drills. Practice with five or six chunks in each lesson and expand learners' vocabulary knowledge.
- Have learners study the chunks and learn how they can be used in various sentences.
- Have them create other sentences using the key chunks.

Role Plays
Reinforce learners' response skills in various business situations through role play exercises. This will enable learners to apply the thematic situations and the skills of global business communication.
- Pair up the class and check out the situation.
- Have learners role play using the background information provided.
- Give feedback on each learner's role play.
- Two role play situations provided.
- Each role play has two roles: **Role A** and **Role B**. Each role has **three tasks** to act on.

Business Issue & Discussion
Provide opportunities to share learners' personal experience, ideas, and opinions more in depth.
- Have learners read the short passage provided and find out which problem or controversial issue is in it.
- Based on what they read, have learners talk about the discussion questions.
- Depending on the level of the class, learners can be divided into two opposing groups to debate the issue.

Business Skills
Reinforce learners' speaking abilities and develop essential business skills, such as presentation skills, meeting skills, negotiation skills, and business writing skills.
- Have learners read a passage about a topic and complete the task as a pair or group work.
- Encourage learners to follow the three things below:
  1. **Reading & Understanding** - Ask learners to read a short passage
  2. **Task** - Ensure they understand the task and what to do. Then, have them complete the task.
  3. **Useful Expressions** - Remind learners to use the useful expressions while they do the task.

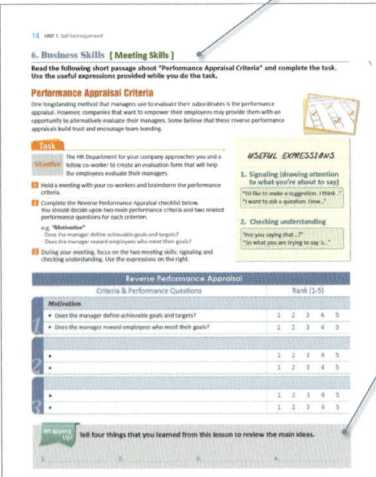

Wrapping Up!
Recall what learners have learned from each lesson by having them call out words that instantly come to their minds.
- Ask each learner to call out a word to the class.
- Ask them why they recall the words and what they learned.

III. Case Study

Each unit includes a Case Study. The Case Studies are based on realistic business situations and problems. They will encourage learners to develop communication skills and problem solving skills by giving them opportunities to practice in realistic business situations.

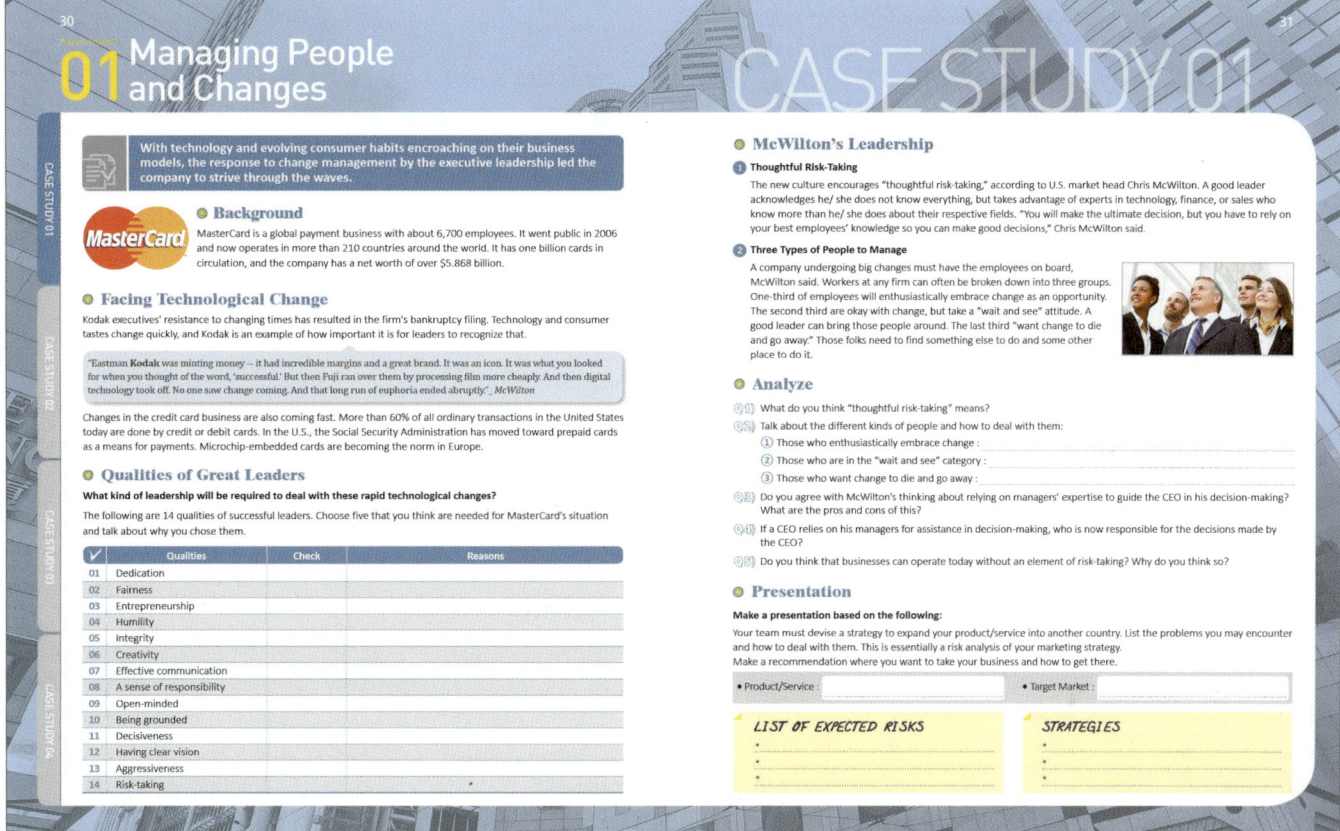

Background Information
Have learners read and understand the background information about the company.

Discussion
Have learners complete an activity that encourages them to think about the problem the company faced and how the problem could be addressed.
- Pair up or make groups to talk about the problem the company had.
- Encourage learners to think about how the company could solve the problem.

Analyze
Encourage learners to talk about the real strategies and how effective they were.
- Have learners read a short passage regarding the strategies the company adopted to solve the problems.
- Ask learners some questions related to the passage and discuss more in depth.

Presentation
Have learners deliver a presentation with a similar situation to the case study.
- Give learners a situation that is similar to the case they studied.
- Have learners complete the task and make a presentation in front of their classmates.

CONTENTS

Unit 1. Self Management

Lesson Title	Learning Objectives	Language Practice	Business Skills	Page
Lesson 01 **Career & Success**	- to define what factors made a job successful - to assess your own and your co-workers' performance	· call the shots · (be) pressed for time/money · around the corner · ascend the corporate ladder · (be) tied up with	Meeting Skills Performance Appraisal Criteria	10
Lesson 02 **Time Management**	- to explain routine jobs and how to handle unexpected ones - to use time effectively and work wisely	· automated process · crunch time · contingency plan · face constraints · strive for	Presentation Skills Time Matrix	15
Lesson 03 **Leadership & Management Style**	- to discuss the roles and qualities of good business leaders - to discuss management and communication styles	· buy out · front office · all-time low · top brass · downward spiral	Meeting Skills Empowerment	20
Lesson 04 **Stress Management**	- to discuss the causes of stress and get some advice to solve problems - to make suggestions to colleagues about how to deal with stress	· clean slate · stride in technology · bank on · get to (somebody) · gains in efficiency	Business Writing Skills Conflict Management Style	25
CASE STUDY	[MasterCard] Managing People and Changes With technology and evolving consumer habits encroaching on their business models, the response to change management by the executive leadership led the company to strive through the waves.			30

Unit 2. Project Management

Lesson Title	Learning Objectives	Language Practice	Business Skills	Page
Lesson 05 **Budgeting**	- to explain the budget, expected expenditure, and expected profit of a new project - to discuss economic situations and financial indicators	· time and cost overruns · debt ceiling · dearth of information · sunk cost · fine-tune · budget buster	Presentation Skills Talking about Projection in Graph Form	32
Lesson 06 **Production Management**	- to report the process and the status of a project and production - to communicate with business partners or outsourcing agents effectively	· lean manufacturing · sweep the globe · brutal economy · ahead of the trend · swings in the stock market · production run	Meeting Skills Persuasion	37
Lesson 07 **Monitoring & Feedback**	- to discuss and learn how to give feedback - to explain problems and learn how to deal with complaints	· common ground · feed off the energy · cut to the chase · pump up · avail (oneself) · tackle a problem	Business Writing Skills Electronic Memo & Purpose Statement	42
Lesson 08 **Risk Management**	- to discuss everyday risk and uncertainty in business - to talk about alternative options and make the best business decision	· winnow out · anemic demand · trade embargoes · due diligence · blind spots · full scope	Presentation Skills Risk Management	47
CASE STUDY	[DuPont] Moving Ahead during Turbulent Times The CEO sets up four principles in order to maintain the company's stability throughout the global financial crisis.			52

Unit 3. Business Strategy

Lesson Title	Learning Objectives	Language Practice	Business Skills	Page
Lesson 09 **Strategic Planning**	- to explain future plans and share the vision and mission of a company - to discuss how to increase business flexibility	· drill down on the data · scale-up operations · core customer · price points · local preference · enter a market	**Meeting Skills** Debate: Good or Bad Vision and Mission Statements	54
Lesson 10 **Strategic Analysis**	- to discuss the weakness and strength of a company in the global market - to explain opportunities and threats to extending a business	· go around in circles · kick-off meeting · data-driven strategy · ahead of the curve · run a pilot program · articulate a strategy	**Business Writing Skills** SWOT Analysis	59
Lesson 11 **International Commerce**	- to clarify the gap between two parties and make adjustments - to discuss contract conditions, bargain, and learn how to reach an agreement	· window of opportunity · task force · think tank · first mover advantage · capitalize on · turn a profit	**Negotiation Skills** Active Listening in Negotiations	64
Lesson 12 **International Markets**	- to discuss the fierce competition of markets and consumers' needs - to explain how to attract attention and promote sales	· advent of technology · head-to-head · be on guard against · on the horizon · attack plan · hot-seller	**Telephone Skills** Understanding the International Market	69
CASE STUDY	**[Orascom Telecom Holding]** Out of Africa: The Egyptian Telecom's Challenge An Egyptian company's strategy of jumping into the global market is proving that it is never too late to go global.			74

Unit 4. Conflict Resolution

Lesson Title	Learning Objectives	Language Practice	Business Skills	Page
Lesson 13 **Communication Breakdown**	- to define the important factors of a good communicator - to discuss how to handle a problem when communication breaks down	· generation gap · stumbling block · down to earth · fall flat · preconceived notions · try one's luck	**Feedback Skills** Constructive Criticism	76
Lesson 14 **Mediation & Resolution**	- to specify the different points of view and understand how to keep good relations - to know how to invite a third party's objective view	· talk in circles · tilt the discussion · a balancing act · a de facto leader · make compromises · win respect	**Communication Skills in Mediation** The Mediator Hat	81
Lesson 15 **Cross-cultural Differences**	- to specify the cultural differences and barriers to communication - to become more aware of cultural etiquette and become more open-minded	· see eye-to-eye · crash course · cultural cue · social fabric · miss the mark · small talk	**Presentation Skills** Training Others	86
Lesson 16 **Business Ethics**	- to exchange opinions about business ethics and morals - to discuss real cases related to ethics and indicate the right and wrong	· fudge the number · rein in · moral fiber · raise a red flag · moral compass · screen for · gray area	**Meeting Skills** Chairing a Meeting	91
CASE STUDY	**[McDonald's]** McDonald's Conquers the Land of Haute Cuisine How McDonald's entered the French market successfully, struggling through social and cultural controversy with sound resolutions.			96

UNIT 1. Self Management

Lesson 01
Career & Success

Learning Objectives

Upon completion of this lesson, you will be able to...
» define what factors made a job successful
» assess your own and your co-workers' performance

"The only place where success comes before work is in the dictionary."
_ Vidal Sassoon

"Develop success from failures. Discouragement and failure are two of the surest stepping stones to success."
_ Dale Carnegie

"Success is not final, failure is not fatal: It is the courage to continue that counts."
– Winston Churchill

1. Warm Up Activities

A Talk about the following questions.

01. What are your main responsibilities at work?
02. How does your daily routine support your year-end goal?
03. Do you have the right skill set for the job?
04. How do you feel about the relationship between promotion and salary?

B Discuss motivation and performance.

01 Which of the following would motivate you to work harder? Choose your top three and rank them in order of priority. Explain your priorities.

- ☐ bonus system
- ☐ working for a successful company
- ☐ more responsibility
- ☐ promotion opportunities
- ☐ perks or fringe benefits
- ☐ work environment

02 The following are Key Performance Indicator (KPI) examples that are used in real-life scenarios. What are the indicators of your job performance? Please think of two and explain.

- ☑ Volume of tasks completed
- ☑ Percentage of overdue processes
- ☑ Number of complaints received within the measurement period
- ☑ Customer satisfaction rate with service provided

Indicators of your performance
1. ....
2. ....

Fill in the blanks with the correct words

- [ ] meticulous
- [ ] expedite
- [ ] assessment
- [ ] micromanage
- [ ] autonomous
- [ ] fringe benefits
- [ ] golden handshake
- [ ] delegate

1. the process of making a judgment or forming an opinion : ....
2. something that you get in addition to your salary; perk : ....
3. to control every small detail : ....
4. detailed; detail-oriented : ....
5. independent and able to make one's own decisions : ....
6. a large amount of money given to a senior manager in a company when he or she leaves the job : ....
7. to speed up the process : ....
8. to give others the assignment : ....

2. Dialogue   Practice the dialogue and answer the questions.

Time for Employee Reviews

John Long time, no talk, Brian. How is your new project treating you?

Brian I've been all tied up with the project. Our team is currently working so hard to get the best results.

John Are you aware that employee evaluations are around the corner?

Brian Yes. That's why we are so pressed for time. Sometimes I need to call the shots to expedite the process even if I don't feel like doing that.

John The results must affect the team-achievement assessment this year. But just be sure not to micromanage every detail of the process.

Brian I agree that employees with workplace autonomy are more productive. Thus, I put more emphasis on what kind of benefits they can earn at the end in reward for their effort.

John Sometimes the more responsibility you delegate to staff, the better. Your team can expect better incentives and more effective fringe benefits next year.

Brian Our team members still recognize that our company has a performance-based wage system as well.

John As a team leader, though, you could expect to ascend the corporate ladder more swiftly

A Situation
Summarize the situation in your own words.

B Questions
1. What are John and Brian talking about?
2. Like Brian, are you currently working on an important project? What kind? How much do the results influence your progress up the career ladder?
3. When was the last employee review in your company? How did it go?
4. What are your goals for the next year? What are the measurable outcomes of these goals? How will you grade performance?

3. Language Practice

Guess the meaning of each chunk and create a new sentence.

1 call the shots

e.g. My supervisor often calls the shots regarding decisions or rules his subordinates must follow.

:

2 (be) pressed for time/money

e.g. I was pressed for time and money to finish this project by this month.

:

3 around the corner

e.g. Never quit; success might be right around the corner.

:

4 ascend the corporate ladder

e.g. He is ascending the corporate ladder quite rapidly.

:

5 (be) tied up with

e.g. I will be tied up with meetings all day.

:

4. Role Plays

Look at each situation and role play with your partner.

A Performance Appraisals

The company recently completed performance appraisals to evaluate its current workforce and make several key promotions. The Vice President, Robert, calls the Director of Sales, Chris, to discuss promotions he would like to make within the sales team. However, Chris thinks the wrong people are being promoted and wants to eliminate performance appraisals.

Role A Vice President, Robert	Role B Director of Sales, Chris
Tells Chris who he wants to promote and why.	Tells Robert why he disagrees with the results of the performance appraisals.
Stresses the importance of performance appraisals.	Tells Robert why performance appraisals can be problematic and inaccurate.
Asks Robert how else employee performance can be assessed.	Suggests better ways to assess employee performance.

Lesson 01 / Career & Success   13

5. Business Issue & Discussion

Read the short passage and discuss the questions in as much detail as possible.

hard working vs. smart working

Consider the following two quotes:

"I do not know anyone who has gotten to the top without hard work. That is the recipe. It will not always get you to the top, but it will get you pretty near."

"Don't tell me how hard you work. Tell me how much you get done."

It has been said that hard work is different than smart work. Hard workers usually attribute their successes to inputs such as the number of hours worked. Typically, they define hard work as working 60 to 80 hours a week, working at home in the evenings and on weekends, and continuously juggling multiple projects in a frantic attempt to get them all done. However, some believe that this is not hard work, but poor time management. They believe in utilizing one's strengths and skills to work smartly and balancing one's work with one's personal life.

① Do you consider yourself a hard worker or a smart worker?

② What are some advantages and disadvantages to each style?

③ Which quote do you agree with?

④ Which type of employee do you think is most likely to get promoted? Why?

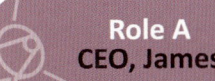 **The Best Candidate**

One of the company's clients recently offered a big project. James, the CEO, will be responsible for assembling a project task force. Eric, one of the employees, approaches James and volunteers to head the project. He wants to express his sincere interest in the opportunity and show that he is confident in his ability to lead the team.

Role A CEO, James	Role B Volunteer, Eric
Would like to know about Eric's past job performance and specific accomplishments.	Asks about the required skills and knowledge, and then expresses his interest in the position.
Asks about the skills and special abilities that Eric has and how they will contribute to the project.	Asks about the benefits that can be gained through the project.
Emphasizes the importance of the project and how it could affect his career path.	Emphasizes the things he can contribute as team leader.

UNIT 1. Self Management

6. Business Skills [Meeting Skills]

Read the following short passage about "Performance Appraisal Criteria" and complete the task. Use the useful expressions provided while you do the task.

Performance Appraisal Criteria

One longstanding method that managers use to evaluate their subordinates is the performance appraisal. However, companies that want to empower their employees may provide them with an opportunity to alternatively evaluate their managers. Some believe that these reverse performance appraisals build trust and encourage team bonding.

Task

Situation: The HR Department for your company approaches you and a fellow co-worker to create an evaluation form that will help the employees evaluate their managers.

1. Hold a meeting with your co-workers and brainstorm the performance criteria.

2. Complete the Reverse Performance Appraisal checklist below. You should decide upon two main performance criteria and two related performance questions for each criterion.

   e.g. *"Motivation"*
   - Does the manager define achievable goals and targets?
   - Does the manager reward employees who meet their goals?

3. During your meeting, focus on the two meeting skills: signaling and checking understanding. Use the expressions on the right.

USEFUL EXPRESSIONS

1. Signaling (drawing attention to what you're about to say)

"I'd like to make a suggestion. I think…"
"I want to ask a question. How…"

2. Checking understanding

"Are you saying that…?"
"So what you are trying to say is…"

Reverse Performance Appraisal

Criteria & Performance Questions	Rank (1-5)
1. Motivation	
▸ Does the manager define achievable goals and targets?	1 2 3 4 5
▸ Does the manager reward employees who meet their goals?	1 2 3 4 5
2.	
▸	1 2 3 4 5
▸	1 2 3 4 5
3.	
▸	1 2 3 4 5
▸	1 2 3 4 5

Wrapping Up! Tell four things that you learned from this lesson to review the main ideas.

1. .... 2. .... 3. .... 4. ....

UNIT 1. Self Management

Lesson 02
Time Management

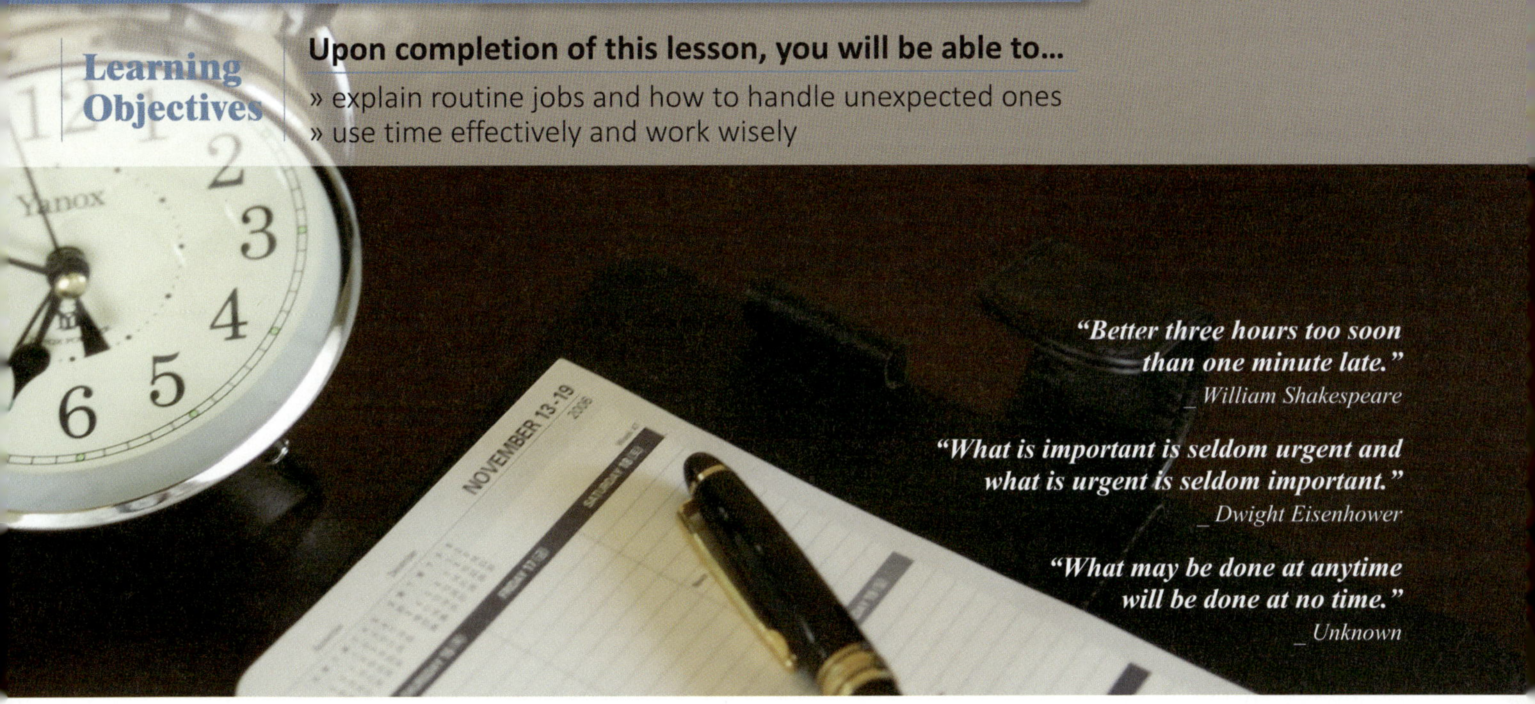

Learning Objectives

Upon completion of this lesson, you will be able to...
» explain routine jobs and how to handle unexpected ones
» use time effectively and work wisely

"Better three hours too soon than one minute late."
_ William Shakespeare

"What is important is seldom urgent and what is urgent is seldom important."
_ Dwight Eisenhower

"What may be done at anytime will be done at no time."
_ Unknown

1. Warm Up Activities

A Talk about your experience.

Which of the following do you think are the biggest timewasters at work? Check them and explain your answers from your experience.

- ☐ Telephone
- ☐ Paperwork
- ☐ Meetings
- ☐ Indecision
- ☐ Procrastination
- ☐ Drop-in visitors
- ☐ Not saying "no"

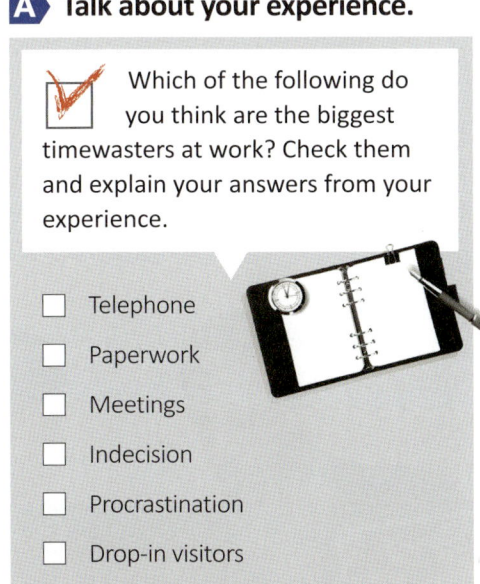

B Discuss the following questions.

01 *Procrastination,* putting off work repeatedly, tends to ruin the work environment and frustrate many workers. How do you deal with procrastination?

02 *"Life hacks"* is a term that refers to productivity tips and tricks that make you more effective at getting things done. Do you have any techniques that improve your lifestyle or make you a more effective worker?

03 *Crunch Time* refers to the final minutes of a sports game in which decisive action is necessary in order to pull off a victory. It also refers to any period in which time is running out to meet the deadline, so utmost and sometimes frantic effort becomes necessary. Have you ever faced a "crunch time"? Why did it happen? How often does it happen?

UNIT 1. Self Management

Fill in the blanks with the correct words

- ☐ consolidate
- ☐ constraint
- ☐ contingency
- ☐ persistent
- ☐ prioritize
- ☐ procrastinate
- ☐ punctual
- ☐ tardy

1. to determine task order according to importance : ....
2. continuing in a course of action or belief despite opposition : ....
3. happening or doing something at the agreed or proper time : ....
4. to delay or postpone doing something : ....
5. delaying or delayed beyond the right or expected time : ....
6. possible future event or circumstance : ....
7. to combine a number of things together into a more coherent whole : ....
8. a limitation or restriction : ....

2. Dialogue   Practice the dialogue and answer the questions.

Striving for the Deadline

Allen Hi, Marcus, how are you dealing with the impending deadline? Are you in serious crunch time?

Marcus For sure! As you know, I tend to be a perfectionist, so being punctual is difficult

Allen No doubt, I can relate. Really, all of us face constraints, so we just need to be persistent and prioritize. Also, I have learned to exploit a few "life hacks" taking advantage of some new tech apps and lifestyle tricks.

Marcus I like what you say! That reminds me... I have been trying to learn how to consolidate my tasks and even automate some processes.

Allen I agree! It seems that most procrastination is half the cause of all crises. Hey, let's talk to the boss about crowdsourcing our data gathering.

Marcus That's a great idea; it might save us time. However, we can't really avoid those unfortunate contingencies that tend to pop-up.

Allen Quite right! What's amusing is that sometimes workers perform best in an urgent situation.

Marcus Well, urgency or no urgency, you know our boss loathes the tardy worker. Plus, nobody truly has job security these days!

Allen Well, I guess to contribute to the group, each person should strive for his own personal best. So, lets get back to work!

A Situation
Summarize the situation in your own words.
....
....

B Questions
1. Allen complains that being a perfectionist makes being punctual difficult? Do you agree with him?
2. Why do humans tend to procrastinate? What are some of the best methods to deal with procrastination?

3. Language Practice

Guess the meaning of each chunk and create a new sentence.

1 automated process

e.g. Whenever I spot a repetitive and iterative task, I set up to an automated process.

:

2 crunch time

e.g. Crunch time is often called do-or-die time; the job must get done.

:

3 contingency plan

e.g. Many companies have a contingency plan for what to do should the undesirable become reality.

:

4 face constraints

e.g. Since every situation faces time constraints, it is best to be a punctual and steady worker.

:

5 strive for

e.g. To strive for perfection through validated routines is one way to make the seemingly impossible become possible.

:

4. Role Plays

Look at each situation and role play with your partner.

A Time Management in an Interview Setting

You are interviewing for a management position. In the first part of the interview, the interviewer poses several questions regarding your time management skills.

Role A Interviewer	Role B Interviewee
Asks about how you manage the time of your subordinates and what you do if someone is preventing you from accomplishing your tasks.	Explain how you handle work that involves others, how you manage teams, and how you delegate your tasks.
Asks about how you handle a large workload and how you prioritize tasks.	Explain how you divide your time and how you determine which tasks are urgent/important.
Asks how you determine what is a reasonable amount of time for a task.	Explain how you assign time to each of your tasks.

Conflicting Deadlines

On April 5th, two clients approach a manufacturer with production requests. The deadline for each is May 5th. Client A has been with the company for 15 years and represents 2% of the company's orders. Client B has been with the company for one year and represents 10% of the company's orders. The Plant Manager is worried that he will not be able to meet both deadlines. He calls the Vice President.

Role A Plant Manager, Raj	Role B Vice President, Steve
Expresses his concern about the dual deadlines.	Asks if there is a way that he can fulfill both orders on time.
Explains his plan for fulfilling both orders on time.	Tells the Plant Manager that his plan may not be possible. Asks the Plant Manager which deadline he feels is more important and why.
Tells the Vice President which deadline he feels is more flexible.	Prioritizes the deadlines and gives instructions to the Plant Manager.

5. Business Issue & Discussion

Read the short passage and discuss the questions in as much detail as possible.

Targets and Milestones

The CFO of Lehman's Bookstore recently held a planning meeting with two of his branch managers. The branches currently have similar monthly profits and customer traffic. Each branch averages around $20,000/month profit and customer traffic hovers around 50,000 visits/month. The regional manager asked the branch managers to set profit and customer traffic targets and milestones.

Manager A set his targets at $21,000/month profit and 51,000 customer visits/month in 12 months. He chose profit milestones of $20,200, $20,400, $20,600, and $20,800, and customer traffic milestones of 50,200, 50,400, 50,600, and 50,800 visits/month. Manager B set his targets at $60,000/month profit and 80,000 customer visits/month by the end of six months. He chose a profit milestone of $40,000 and a customer traffic milestone of 65,000 visits/month.

The CFO was very upset about how his managers selected their targets and milestones.

❶ Why did the CFO get upset? With whom do you think he was most disappointed?

❷ What are more appropriate targets and milestones? Talk about some good guidelines to follow when setting targets and milestones.

❸ Do you think targets and milestones should be risky or not risky? Why?

6. Business Skills [Presentation Skills]

Read the following short passage about "Time Matrix" and complete the task. Use the useful expressions provided while you deliver the presentation.

Time Matrix

Great time management requires prioritizing tasks based on their importance and urgency. Important tasks often lead to the achievement of your own goals, whereas urgent tasks demand immediate attention and are associated with the achievement of another's goals.

If a task was important and urgent, you would use all possible resources to complete the task immediately. If it was important but not urgent, you would give it an end date and commit to working on it. If it was unimportant but urgent, you would delegate the task to his staff. If it was unimportant and not urgent, most likely it could be ignored or deferred.

	URGENCY	
IMPORTANCE	URGENT AND IMPORTANT (1)	IMPORTANT BUT NOT URGENT (2)
	URGENT BUT NOT IMPORTANT (3)	NEITHER URGENT NOR IMPORTANT (4)

Task

1. Choose a company and a position within that company that you want to hold (e.g. Customer Service Representative for United Airlines).
   - Company: _____
   - Your Position: _____

2. Think of plausible tasks that your position might entail. Based on how important or urgent you believe them to be, put them into the time matrix above.

3. Present your quadrant to the class, describing each task and the reasons for your classifications.
   Deliver the presentation by using the expressions provided in the box.

USEFUL EXPRESSIONS

1 Meaning of the Visual
"This chart/graph shows…"
"This chart/graph illustrates…"
"This chart/graph demonstrates…"
"This chart/graph refers to…"
"As you can see, this is…"

2 Focusing Attention
"I'd like to draw your attention to…"
"One of the most important aspects of this is…"

3 Explanation
"The reason for this is…"
"What this tells you is that…"

Wrapping Up!
Tell four things that you learned from this lesson to review the main ideas.

1. _____ 2. _____ 3. _____ 4. _____

UNIT 1. Self Management

Lesson 03

Leadership & Management Style

Learning Objectives

Upon completion of this lesson, you will be able to...
» discuss the roles and qualities of good business leaders
» discuss management and communication styles

"Never tell people how to do things. Tell them what to do and they will surprise you with their ingenuity."
_ General George Patton

"I start with the premise that the function of leadership is to produce more leaders, not more followers."
_ Ralph Nader

1. Warm Up Activities

A Qualities of Great Leaders

 Which of the following do you think are the best qualities of a great leader? Check three qualities and explain your opinion.

- [ ] Charisma
- [ ] Decisiveness
- [ ] Having clear vision
- [ ] Taking the initiative
- [ ] Leading by example
- [ ] Effective communication skills
- [ ] Smart people networking

B Discuss the following questions.

1 ***Authoritarian*** is generally used to describe a person who controls everything and forces others to obey strict rules and laws. Authoritarian can also refer to such controlling actions. Some leaders are considered very authoritarian, whereas others are more democratic. Which style of leader do you prefer?

2 ***As bottom-up feedback,*** many CEOs want to be evaluated by their subordinates. How do you feel about such an idea? If you had to give your boss some feedback, how would you prefer to do it: face-to-face in a private chat or through anonymous feedback?

3 ***Emotional intelligence*** is the ability to identify, assess, and control the emotions of oneself, of others, and of groups. Some CEOs have much technical knowledge.
Other CEOs have high emotional intelligence, which means that they are great at understanding and getting along with people. Do you value technical knowledge or emotional knowledge more in a leader? How often does it happen?

Lesson 03 / Leadership & Management Style   21

Fill in the blanks with the correct words

- ☐ audacious
- ☐ gutsy
- ☐ shrewd
- ☐ charisma
- ☐ empathy
- ☐ morale
- ☐ polarizing

1. attractiveness and charm that can persuade others : ....
2. having or showing courage or determination : ....
3. having sharp power of judgment : ....
4. the ability to understand and share the feelings of another : ....
5. the confidence, enthusiasm, and discipline of a person or group : ....
6. to be divisive and create opposition or resentment : ....
7. willing to take bold risks; bold : ....

2. Dialogue   Practice the dialogue and answer the questions.

Turnaround

Isabelle Well, if we get bought out by our competitor, it is probably because we have not made enough gutsy decisions.

Jasper True. On the one hand, our boss supposedly has a reputation for being shrewd, but we could use more charisma and action from the top brass, especially the CEO.

Isabelle Not to mention, my friend in sales says that the front office feels like upper management in the company is very polarizing in making resources available.

Jasper Yep, it seems morale is at an all-time low. However, let's not give up hope yet!

Isabelle I think that we should make some audacious moves to reverse this downward spiral. Really, it is now or never, if we want to remain independent.

Jasper That's right, we need to be bold, daring, and inventive if we want to recoup losses and gain traction in this market.

Isabelle Really, mentality and team spirit are a big part of an enterprise.

Jasper Yeah, I have learned never to undervalue the importance of leadership.

A Situation
Summarize the situation in your own words.

B Questions
1. Isabelle mentions that their company is on a downward spiral, which means that one problem has led to another. What do you think is a good way to stop a negative trend in events within a company?
2. What do you think is a better remedy for turning a company around: practical work that is very simple and direct, or very bold plans that might cause disruption but could also create large increase?
3. How much do you value charisma in a leader? Do you think that charisma can be taught, or is it a natural quality that people are born with?

3. Language Practice

Guess the meaning of each chunk and create a new sentence.

1 buy out
e.g. To become an even bigger company, we decided to buy out our rival by purchasing all their public stock.
:

2 front office
e.g. As a salesman, I am so glad to be a part of the front office because that is where you get to meet the most costumers.
:

3 all-time low
e.g. Just as it seemed that the economy could not get any worse, news of the oil spill sank economic performance to a new all-time low.
:

4 top brass
e.g. It is not my goal to be a part of the top brass because I get my esteem from my ability to create, not from my ability to command others.
:

5 downward spiral
e.g. The series of setbacks sent us into a downward spiral where it seemed that we could not get into the proper position.
:

4. Role Plays

Look at each situation and role play with your partner.

A Setting Goals

Mike is the manager of a real estate agency, and he just hired a new real estate agent. She doesn't have much experience in real estate, but she has worked as a saleswoman before. She comes to Mike and asks him to set some short-term and long-term goals for her.

> **Tip:** *The manager should follow the SMART Goal Setting Strategy (Specific, Measurable, Attainable, Realistic, Timely) to define her goals.*

- Asks Mike to set some short- and long-term goals for her.
- Asks Mike to set forth timeframes for the goals.
- Tells Mike about the goals she will set for herself and when she hopes to achieve them.

Role A
Real Estate Agent, Karen

- Provides Karen with specific, measurable, attainable, and realistic goals.
- Sets the timeframes and then asks her if she has any of her own goals.
- Responds to Karen's personal goals and explains whether he thinks they are reasonable. Tells her how he can help her reach them.

Role B
Manager, Mike

Lesson 03 / Leadership & Management Style   23

B Organizational Structure and Reporting

A reporter at a local newspaper is writing an article about Peach Computers, one of the leading computer companies in the country. He arranges a phone interview with the CEO of the company. One of the main topics that the reporter addresses is the company's organizational structure. Because of the company's global expansion, it recently reorganized from a functional structure to a matrix structure.

Role A — Reporter	Role B — CEO
Praises the company's success and inquires about the company's recent reorganization.	Explains what prompted the reorganization and why the functional structure no longer worked.
Asks about each structure and why they chose a matrix structure instead of a divisional structure.	Details the advantages and disadvantages of each structure and why they decided to make the change.
Asks if he encountered any problems during the change.	Details some of the initial problems that occurred, but then highlights the subsequent successes.

5. Business Issue & Discussion

Read the short passage and discuss the questions in as much detail as possible.

Management Style

One of a manager's biggest difficulties can be to get his or her team members to collaborate and commit to the process. In this regard, a manager is faced with a decision—to employ a top-down or bottom-up management style. In top-down management, the decisions are made at the higher levels of the organization and filter down through the ranks. Conversely, in the bottom-up approach, team members set the goals and are then responsible for achieving such goals.

bottom-up management style.

1. Which management style do you think is most effective?

2. Are there certain industries or situations that are better suited to a particular style? Should management style be task-dependent or employee-dependent?

3. Is there a way to combine both of these styles?

6. Business Skills [Meeting Skills]

Read the following short passage about "Empowerment" and complete the task. Use the useful expressions provided while you do the task.

Empowerment

As a leader, one of your primary goals should be to empower your employees. An effective leader does not micromanage—he or she develops his or her employees' core skills and competencies, gives them the autonomy to make key decisions, and then holds them accountable for their actions. Empowering employees in this fashion creates loyalty, builds morale, grooms employees for the future, and contributes to the overall success of the company.

One of the quickest ways of "disempowering" employees is to react harshly when an employee fails, especially if that employee believed he or she was acting in the best interest of the company. The best thing to do is to find the good in the employee's actions, point out what he or she may not have done correctly in a positive manner, and encourage him or her to do better next time. Below are five rules to follow when an employee makes a mistake, accompanied by phrases that can be used when confronting the employee.

1 Praise people publicly, but scold them privately.
- "(name), could I please see you in my office for a minute?"
- "(name), can you spare some time to speak in my office?"

2 Highlight the error.
- "The problem was that…"
- "Do you see the mistake that you made?"

3 Discuss what the employee should have done instead.
- "I would like to have seen…"
- "What do you think could have been done differently?"

4 Talk about what needs to happen so that the same mistake isn't repeated.
- "Next time, how about…?"
- "What did you learn from this mistake?"

5 Let them know that you are disappointed.
- "I expect more from you. I hope this doesn't happen again."
- "I'm not mad, but I'm a little disappointed. Let's try harder next time."

Task

Situation: An accounting manager recently requested his accounting clerk to make a bank transfer of $16,000 from the company's savings account to its checking account so that they would have enough money to write checks for that month's bills. The accounting clerk forgot one of the zeroes and made a transfer of $1,600. It is now a week later, and the company is beginning to receive calls from suppliers and clients about the bad checks they received. The accounting clerk is extremely embarrassed and upset.

1. With a partner, take turns acting as the accounting manager and accounting clerk.

2. The accounting manager should follow the five rules and use the language tips provided to explain the clerk's error, help him learn from his mistake, and empower him to succeed the next time.

Wrapping Up! Tell four things that you learned from this lesson to review the main ideas.

1. _____ 2. _____ 3. _____ 4. _____

UNIT 1. Self Management

Lesson 04
Stress Management

Learning Objectives

Upon completion of this lesson, you will be able to...
» discuss the causes of stress and get some advice to solve problems
» make suggestions to colleagues about how to deal with stress

"Much of the stress that people feel doesn't come from having too much to do. It comes from not finishing what they've started."
_ David Allen

"There are two ways of meeting difficulties: You alter the difficulties or you alter yourself to meet them."
_ Phyllis Bottome

1. Warm Up Activities

A Talk about workplace stress factors.

According to research, the following are the top stress factors in the workplace. Review the list and select the three factors which you think most affect your workplace stress.

- [ ] Low Salary
- [ ] Lack of Opportunity for Advancement
- [ ] A Heavy Workload
- [ ] Unrealistic Job Expectations
- [ ] Long Hours
- [ ] Uncertain or Unclear Job Expectations
- [ ] Work Interference with Personal or Family Time
- [ ] Job Insecurity
- [ ] Lack of Participation in Decision-making
- [ ] Inflexible Hours
- [ ] Commuting
- [ ] Problems with Supervisor
- [ ] Problems with Co-workers
- [ ] Personal Life Interfering with Work

B Discuss the following questions.

Some companies are going to far lengths in order to fight workplace stress.

1 *Bringing your dog to work* can improve collaboration and reduce stress, and many firms allow dogs at work.
The thinking is that having a dog is fun and uplifting, so the workers will naturally be upbeat in response to the dog. What is your reaction to this policy? Has your company tried anything trendy to fight stress?

2 *Quick breaks* and some fresh air can be a quick way to revive the mind. On the other hand, too many breaks can disrupt momentum. What is your policy on taking breaks? Do you try to make breaks "productive"? How can breaks be both a rest and also a way to get ahead?

Fill in the blanks with the correct words

- ☐ trade-off
- ☐ fatigue
- ☐ downtime
- ☐ clutter
- ☐ barrier
- ☐ momentum
- ☐ burnout / burned out

1. strength or force in a direction due to previous effort and activity : ....
2. free time; personal time away from the office; a short break : ....
3. physical and mental exhaustion and collapse due to prolonged stress : ....
4. weariness or exhaustion : ....
5. something, mental or physical, that blocks, impedes, or separates : ....
6. a confused mass of objects : ....
7. a giving up of one thing in exchange for another; a balancing of factors, all of which are not attainable at the same time : ....

2. Dialogue   Practice the dialogue and answer the questions.

Downtime

Ethan Wow, all these deadlines are really getting to me. I cannot wait to have some quality downtime this weekend.

Jessica I think that if we could just get some momentum going, these problems would not be as big as they now seem.

Ethan Well, we are always facing trade-offs. To get more success requires more sacrifice.

Jessica I'm banking on this new software to create more gains in efficiency.

Ethan For sure, strides in technology have made certain processes faster, but I also feel more information overload.

Jessica I think that to handle my fatigue, it is not going to require any new technology but really some old-fashioned R&R.

Ethan You mean, rest and relaxation? That sounds almost impossible to get these days.

Jessica Too true. It seems each new day just adds to the clutter on my desk, not to speak of the mental clutter I have been feeling these days.

Ethan Even e-mail seems to be just another barrier in the morning before I get to my real work.

Jessica I wish that I could start each quarter with a clean slate.

A Situation
Summarize the situation in your own words.

....

....

B Questions

1. What does Ethan struggle with at work? Do you have any particular struggles with your work day?

2. Have you or your company invested in any new technology lately in the hope that your work will improve? Discuss what you purchased, why you purchased it, and what the results have been so far.

3. Jessica can't wait for a "clean slate." Basically, she likes to start fresh a few times a year. What chances does your job offer you to "start anew" and build something from the start?

3. Language Practice

Guess the meaning of each chunk and create a new sentence.

1 clean slate

e.g. The newly elected president promised that with a clean slate he could start off fresh and not be limited by the previous administration.

:
___

2 stride in technology

e.g. The future envisioned in sci-fi novels and movies depends on consistent and sometimes far-reaching strides in technology.

:
___

3 bank on

e.g. Our company is banking on a new partnership to expose us to more potential customers and greater brand recognition.

:
___

4 get to (somebody)

e.g. The demands of the job were getting to me so much that finally I decided to take a vacation.

:
___

5 gains in efficiency

e.g. By purchasing the new software, our company is looking for noticeable gains in efficiency.

:
___

4. Role Plays

Look at each situation and role play with your partner.

A Work-Life Balance

Steve's boss is a workaholic and thinks that everyone else in the office should be as well. Steve works extremely late hours and on the weekends, creating conflicts in his personal life. Steve has no problem working hard, but feels he can be just as successful working fewer hours, thus restoring harmony to his life. He requests a face-to-face meeting with his boss.

Role A Steve	Role B Steve's Boss
Respectfully tells his boss that he is struggling with the long hours. Details the changes he would like to make.	Reminds Steve about how much there is to do and that they have to work long hours and weekends to get it all done.
Informs his boss that a worker with more balance in his or her life is more productive and more loyal.	Tells Steve that he is worried about the company's success if he works less.
Assures his boss that he can be more productive during his time at work and that he can still meet his goals on time. Demonstrates the benefits to the company.	Requests a compromise. Suggests only working late during crunch times or possibly bringing some work home.

B. Human Resources and Stress Management

The employees at a financial firm are worried about their stress levels and have asked the human resource department to help. Human resources is taking this problem very seriously, as they are worried about health problems and the effects of stress on morale, creativity, productivity, and loyalty. Two members of the human resource department are discussing programs that might mitigate workplace stress.

Role A — HR Employee 1	Role B — HR Employee 2
Suggests building some on-site amenities such as a cafeteria, dry cleaner, post office, or pharmacy.	Worries about the cost of such amenities and asks if his/her team member has any other suggestions.
Suggests providing the employees with memberships to a nearby fitness club and allowing them extra time in the day to exercise.	Likes the idea and then recommends offering some employees the potential to telecommute.
Thinks that they should hold stress management workshops in order to warn employees about the dangers of stress and how to cope with it.	Agrees with him/her. Discusses approaching upper management with the ideas and time frames for implementing the programs.

5. Business Issue & Discussion

Read the short passage and discuss the questions in as much detail as possible.

Organizational Conflict

There are three types of conflict that can exist within an organization—the good, the bad, and the ugly. **Good conflicts** can be healthy and productive, spurring creativity and innovation. **Bad conflicts** result from problems in the organization, such as ill-defined job responsibilities or glitches in the organizational structure. These can be remedied by adjusting the power structure, separating conflict members, further elaborating job descriptions, etc. **Ugly conflicts** are complete disruptions to an organization. Often, they exist for many years, there is a lot of secretive complaining about them, and employees spend little time trying to resolve them, instead focusing on self-preservation.

1. Do you agree that conflicts can be classified in this way? Can conflicts be separated into bad and ugly?

2. Do you think that some conflicts are positive? Discuss some examples of good conflicts and how they can help an organization.

3. What are the best ways to resolve "ugly" conflicts?

6. Business Skills [Business Writing Skills]

Read the following short passage about "Conflict Management Style" and complete the task.
Use the useful expressions provided while you do the task.

Conflict Management Style

Below you will see the Thomas-Killman Conflict Mode Instrument. It defines five conflict management styles based on two dimensions: assertiveness and cooperativeness.

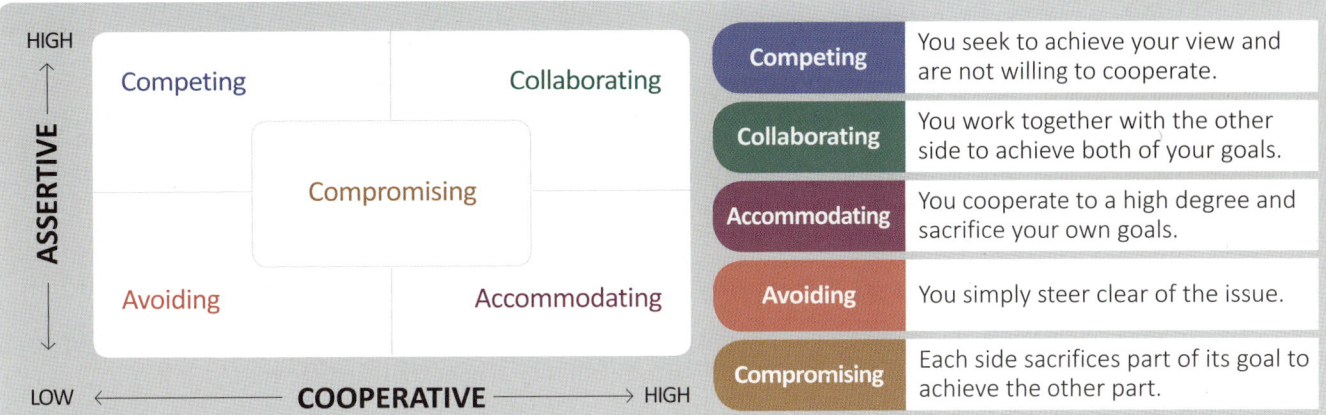

Task

Situation: You are the manager of a clothing factory. You have plans to expand, and your new facility will be built adjacent to a small stream. You receive a letter from a community representative expressing her concern about your expansion, including water pollution, the effect on scenery, noise, etc.

1 Choose one conflict resolution style (other than avoiding).

.... Style

2 Write a short letter for the style that responds to the representative's issue.

USEFUL EXPRESSIONS

1 Being Assertive
- "I have a different opinion. I think that..."
- "You are entitled to your own opinion, and I respect that, but..."
- "This time, we need to..."
- "Let's agree to disagree and move on."

2 Compromising
- "I like both, so let's..."
- "How can we meet both of our needs?"
- "I am willing to compromise on..."
- "I'll meet you halfway."

 **Tell four things that you learned from this lesson to review the main ideas.**

1. .... 2. .... 3. .... 4. ....

01 Managing People and Changes

Business Practice 2

> With technology and evolving consumer habits encroaching on their business models, the response to change management by the executive leadership led the company to strive through the waves.

◎ Background

MasterCard is a global payment business with about 6,700 employees. It went public in 2006 and now operates in more than 210 countries around the world. It has one billion cards in circulation, and the company has a net worth of over $5.868 billion.

◎ Facing Technological Change

Kodak executives' resistance to changing times has resulted in the firm's bankruptcy filing. Technology and consumer tastes change quickly, and Kodak is an example of how important it is for leaders to recognize that.

> "Eastman **Kodak** was minting money -- it had incredible margins and a great brand. It was an icon. It was what you looked for when you thought of the word, 'successful.' But then Fuji ran over them by processing film more cheaply. And then digital technology took off. No one saw change coming. And that long run of euphoria ended abruptly." _ McWilton

Changes in the credit card business are also coming fast. More than 60% of all ordinary transactions in the United States today are done by credit or debit cards. In the U.S., the Social Security Administration has moved toward prepaid cards as a means for payments. Microchip-embedded cards are becoming the norm in Europe.

◎ Qualities of Great Leaders

What kind of leadership will be required to deal with these rapid technological changes?

The following are 14 qualities of successful leaders. Choose five that you think are needed for MasterCard's situation and talk about why you chose them.

✓	Qualities	Check	Reasons
01	Dedication		
02	Fairness		
03	Entrepreneurship		
04	Humility		
05	Integrity		
06	Creativity		
07	Effective communication		
08	A sense of responsibility		
09	Open-minded		
10	Being grounded		
11	Decisiveness		
12	Having clear vision		
13	Aggressiveness		
14	Risk-taking		

CASE STUDY 01

◎ McWilton's Leadership

1 Thoughtful Risk-Taking

The new culture encourages "thoughtful risk-taking," according to U.S. market head Chris McWilton. A good leader acknowledges he/ she does not know everything, but takes advantage of experts in technology, finance, or sales who know more than he/ she does about their respective fields. "You will make the ultimate decision, but you have to rely on your best employees' knowledge so you can make good decisions," Chris McWilton said.

2 Three Types of People to Manage

A company undergoing big changes must have the employees on board, McWilton said. Workers at any firm can often be broken down into three groups. One-third of employees will enthusiastically embrace change as an opportunity. The second third are okay with change, but take a "wait and see" attitude. A good leader can bring those people around. The last third "want change to die and go away." Those folks need to find something else to do and some other place to do it.

◎ Analyze

Q1) What do you think "thoughtful risk-taking" means?

Q2) Talk about the different kinds of people and how to deal with them:
   ① Those who enthusiastically embrace change : ....
   ② Those who are in the "wait and see" category : ....
   ③ Those who want change to die and go away : ....

Q3) Do you agree with McWilton's thinking about relying on managers' expertise to guide the CEO in his decision-making? What are the pros and cons of this?

Q4) If a CEO relies on his managers for assistance in decision-making, who is now responsible for the decisions made by the CEO?

Q5) Do you think that businesses can operate today without an element of risk-taking? Why do you think so?

◎ Presentation

Make a presentation based on the following:

Your team must devise a strategy to expand your product/service into another country. List the problems you may encounter and how to deal with them. This is essentially a risk analysis of your marketing strategy.
Make a recommendation where you want to take your business and how to get there.

• Product/Service : _____   • Target Market : _____

LIST OF EXPECTED RISKS
* ....
* ....
* ....

STRATEGIES
* ....
* ....
* ....

UNIT 2. Project Management

Lesson 05
Budgeting

Learning Objectives

Upon completion of this lesson, you will be able to...
» explain the budget, expected expenditure, and expected profit of a new project
» discuss economic situations and financial indicators

"Changes start occurring when budgets are cut."
_ Ben Horowitz

"A budget is just a method of worrying before you spend money, as well as afterward."
_ Unknown

1. Warm Up Activities

A Discuss the following questions.

1. How does your company decide its budget(s)? How does the company budget affect you and your work throughout the year?

2. A wise investment and money-managing adage is: **"A penny saved is a penny earned."** Could you explain the rationale of this statement? How much do you value it? What kind of effort does your company put forth for tight budgeting?

B Re-anchoring

In setting budgets, planning committees tend to use this year's numbers as a baseline for next year's performance. However, ambitious and strategic workers want to reap the full value of what the market can bear. Therefore, to adjust budgets, some managers try a method called "re-anchoring." To start gauging greater potential, a manager will ask, "What would it take~?" questions, such as:

☑ What would it take to double growth?
☑ What would it take to achieve the same performance with half as much spending?

Try making three of your own budget challenging questions. Then ask them to a partner and imagine responses for each other.

☑ What would it take ....?
☑ What would it take ....?
☑ What would it take ....?

Fill in the blanks with the correct words

- ☐ frugal
- ☐ forecast
- ☐ benchmark
- ☐ leverage
- ☐ panacea
- ☐ inertia
- ☐ dearth
- ☐ tight-fisted

1. a point of reference by which performance can be measured; (sometimes, a standard set by a competitor's success) : ....
2. the tendency of a body to resist acceleration; disinclination to motion, action, or change : ....
3. characterized by or reflecting economy in the use of resources; thrifty : ....
4. to calculate and predict based on analysis and study of available data : ....
5. hypothetical remedy for all diseases or ills : ....
6. power, effectiveness; a resource that allows one to enact or perform; to use to advantage : ....
7. an acute insufficiency : ....
8. unwilling to spend money, mean : ....

2. Dialogue   Practice the dialogue and answer the questions.

Budget Tightening

Emily I am so elated to hear this fabulous news. Let's just say that I am more than cautiously optimistic that we can not only match but exceed all benchmarks from previous Olympics.

Peter I agree that we have the spirit, but do we have the budget? With all these political talks recently about the debt ceiling, I hope that new stadium is not seen as a budget buster.

Emily That's right; now is not the time to be so frugal and tight-fisted! However, we can leverage our net assets and use our inherent strengths coupled with wise resource allocation to make savvy decisions.

Peter Well, we must identify threats that could cause time and cost overruns as well as accurately forecast earned value for the sunk costs.

Emily Well said! A responsible fiscal policy is wise, but we should overcome inertia to build ambitiously. Not that smart design is any sort of panacea for public ills.

Peter For sure! Let's make sure to fine-tune our budget to represent all fixed costs.

Emily Well then, we need to prevent a dearth of information from posing risks.

Peter Basically, we need a seamless plan of action.

A Situation

Summarize the situation in your own words.
....
....

B Questions

1. Peter and Emily talk a lot about time and money. Which resource do you think is more valuable? Can you explain the utility and detriment of each?
2. Do you think being frugal is the same as being tight-fisted?
3. Are you able to compare and contrast short-term costs and value to long-term costs and value?
4. In some projects, good design often costs more at the outset but provides a more meaningful and significant return in the long run. What are your views of design?

3. Language Practice

Guess the meaning of each chunk and create a new sentence.

1 time and cost overruns
e.g. The longer an IT project is supposed to take, the more likely it is to encounter time and cost overruns.
:

2 debt ceiling
e.g. To enforce a strict practice of no more debt, some countries and companies are adopting a debt ceiling.
:

3 dearth of information
e.g. A rational marketplace requires the free-flow of information; however, often there is a dearth of information.
:

4 sunk cost
e.g. When judging profit, risk, and the commitment to an undertaking, you must consider the sunk costs as well as other obligations.
:

5 fine-tune
e.g. To reach your targets and sales goals and make them realistic, it is important to fine-tune them in relation to data at your disposal.
:

6 budget buster
e.g. It could potentially be a budget buster because we don't know how it's going to be paid for.
:

4. Role Plays

Look at each situation and role play with your partner.

A Budget Variance and Estimation

Robotronics Inc. produces three types of toy robots: the Maximus, the Optimus, and the Pegasus. The Sales Manager's third quarter sales budget is shown in Table A. The actual results are shown in Table B. The Senior Vice President would like the Sales Manager to: a) explain the variances; and b) summarize his fourth quarter budget.

TABLE A: BUDGETED FIGURES, 3rd Quarter						
	Sales Units	Price per Unit	Total Sales	*VC per Unit	Total *VC	Contribution Margin
Maximus	12,500	$350	$4,375,000	$175	$2,187,500	$2,187,500
Optimus	37,500	$250	$9,375,000	$140	$5,250,000	$4,125,000
Pegasus	50,000	$150	$7,500,000	$85	$4,250,000	$3,250,000
Total	100,000		$21,250,000		$11,687,500	$9,562,500
TABLE B: ACTUAL FIGURES, 3rd Quarter						
	Sales Units	Price per Unit	Total Sales	*VC per Unit	Total *VC	Contribution Margin
Maximus	8,000	$300	$2,400,000	$220	$1,760,000	$640,000
Optimus	45,000	$275	$12,375,000	$120	$5,400,000	$6,975,000
Pegasus	51,000	$170	$8,670,000	$100	$5,100,000	$3,570,000
Total	104,000		$23,445,000		$12,260,000	$11,185,000

*VC = Variable Costs = Costs that change with the amount produced and include items like wages, utilities, materials used in production, etc. These differ from Fixed Costs (FC), which remain the same regardless of output and include items like rent, advertising, etc.

Role A — Senior Vice President
- Requests that the Sales Manager give an overview of the variances.
- Specifically addresses the Maximus due to the sizable gaps between budgeted and actual figures.
- Asks the Sales Manager to summarize the budget for the fourth quarter and to explain any special considerations.

Role B — Sales Manager
- Provides a summary of the budget variances.
- Discusses the Maximus, but then highlights the success of the Optimus, as well as the Pegasus, which came in close to budget.
- Explains the process by which he/she budgeted for the fourth quarter.

Lesson 05 / Budgeting

B Capital Budgeting

Shake and Burger is considering the purchase of $150,000 of new equipment so that it can expand its menu. The equipment will last seven years, with a *salvage value of $50,000. The new equipment is expected to lead to an increase in cash inflows of $250,000 per year, with outflows of $200,000. The Finance Department evaluated the investment, and now one of its team members must present the investment to a loan officer, who will lend the funds to the company if the investment is attractive.

The loan officer will be looking at three common investment decision criteria:

1. Payback Period (PP) – the required time to recover the cost of the investment; *the shorter the payback period, the better the investment.*
2. Net Present Value (NPV) – the difference between the present value of all the future cash flows of an investment and the amount of the investment; *a positive NPV indicates a good investment.*
3. Internal Rate of Return (IRR) – the interest rate that makes the sum of all cash flows equal to zero; *an investment is attractive if the IRR is higher than the interest rate on another investment with equal risk.*

The Finance Department has come up with the following figures:

1. Payback Period = 3 years
2. Net Present Value = $80,449.57
3. Internal Rate of Return = 16%

Salvage value – the value of the item at the end of its useful life.

Role A — Finance Team Member

Role B — Bank Loan Officer

Role A	Role B
Explains the nature of the project and the assumptions they made when evaluating it.	Asks how they got their estimates for cash inflows and outflows.
Explains their budgeted figures.	Asks him/her to explain the project in terms of PP, NPV, and IRR. Tells him that the bank requires a 14% rate of return.
Highlights the project's viability based on its PP, NPV, and IRR.	Makes a decision about the loan.

5. Business Issue & Discussion

Read the short passage and discuss the questions in as much detail as possible.

Budgeting and Innovation

Running a business requires planning for the future. Thus, in some form or another, most businesses use budgets. Budgets draw a financial roadmap for an organization and help the company learn about itself and its external business environment. Budgets also limit expenditures by holding managers accountable for their project costs.

However, the biggest criticism of budgets is that they stifle innovation. The Beyond Budgeting Round Table (BBRT) argues that budgeting suppresses trust and empowerment and, therefore, innovation. Indeed, entrepreneurial managers can find themselves in hot water for incurring costs on projects that were not included in their budgets. Budgeting, consequently, discourages risk taking and "big picture" strategies, hindering innovation and change.

① Do you think the BBRT's stance is accurate?

② How can an organization alter its budgeting and review procedures so that they do not hinder innovation?

③ Are there any other disadvantages to budgeting? What are its advantages? Do you think a company can survive without budgeting?

6. Business Skills [Presentation Skills]

Learn the useful expressions for describing graphs or chart and complete the task.

Talking about Projections in Graph Form

When presenting a budget graph, two of the things that you will have to address are the trends and time horizons. Below are a few ways of discussing your projections.

1 Trends	**2** Time Horizons
- "…declines rapidly…" - "…reaches a peak…" - "…drops slowly…" - "…falls into the red…" (meaning "becomes negative") - "…fluctuates mildly…"	- "By the end of (time horizon), I/we expect to see (line item)…" - "It is anticipated that at the end of (time horizon) (line item) will…" - "My/Our projections show that (line item) will…in (time horizon)." - "(Line item) should…over the next (time horizon)." - "Over the course of the next (time horizon), (line item) will…"

Task

You have prepared a cash budget and an accompanying graph (shown below) for the upcoming year showing the cash on hand at the end of each quarter. Present your budget to management so that they can review your projections.

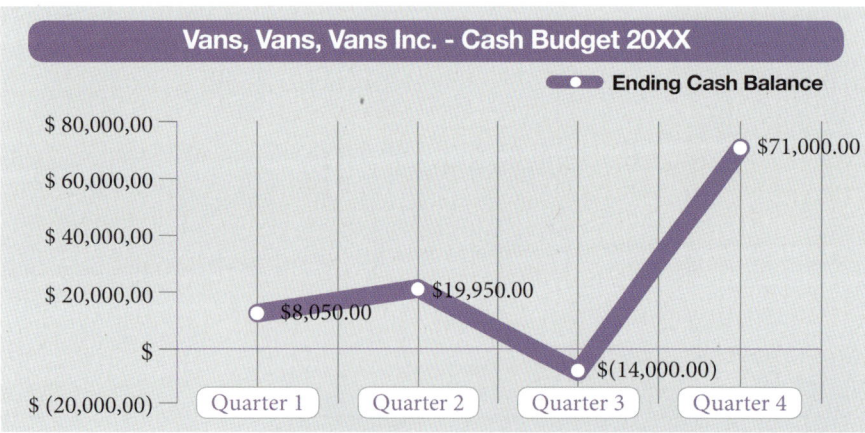

	Quarter 1	Quarter 2	Quarter 3	Quarter 4
Beginning Cash Balance	$30,000.00	$8,050.00	$19,950.00	$(14,000.00)
Sources of Cash				
Accounts Receivable Collected	$201,000.00	$243,000.00	$354,000.00	$528,000.00
Land Sales	$-	$-	$15,000.00	$-
Total Cash Available	$201,000.00	$243,000.00	$369,000.00	$528,000.00
Uses of Cash				
Direct Materials	$(46,700.00)	$(37,300.00)	$(54,000.00)	$(67,000.00)
Direct Labor	$(67,500.00)	$(76,500.00)	$(126,000.00)	$(180,000.00)
Manufacturing Overhead	$(45,000.00)	$(51,000.00)	$(84,000.00)	$(120,000.00)
Selling and Administrative	$(33,750.00)	$(38,250.00)	$(63,000.00)	$(90,000.00)
Equipment Purchases	$-	$(20,000.00)	$(56,000.00)	$-
Total Uses of Cash	$(192,950.00)	$(223,050.00)	$(383,000.00)	$(457,000.00)
Ending Cash Balance	$8,050.00	$19,950.00	$(14,000.00)	$71,000.00

Wrapping Up!

Tell four things that you learned from this lesson to review the main ideas.

1. _____
2. _____
3. _____
4. _____

UNIT 2. Project Management

Lesson 06

Production Management

Learning Objectives

Upon completion of this lesson, you will be able to...
» report the process and the status of a project and production
» communicate with business partners or outsourcing agents effectively

"Watch the little things; a small leak will sink a great ship."
_ Benjamin Franklin

"Almost all quality improvement comes via simplification of design, manufacturing, layout, processes, and procedures."
_ Tom Peters

"A bad system will beat a good person every time."
_ W. Edwards Deming

1. Warm Up Activities

A. Talk about future development.

The following are supposedly the key features of future development. Give an example of how your company has improved in any of these five areas.

☐ shorter production runs
☐ higher design
☐ low labor cost
☐ natural resources
☐ customization

B. Discuss the following questions.

1. Technology development: Robots and robotics are increasingly becoming a part of the manufacturing process of new goods. Some people see robots as a growth model for precision and low-cost labor. Others see robots and machines as replacing humans and thereby leaving some people without jobs. What is your opinion about the role of machines and robots in human life, especially the economy? Do you see robots more as an aid or a threat?

2. Globalization is forcing businesses to make cost-saving decisions by reducing operating costs. So, many countries are setting up facilities (e.g. factories, call centers) in countries that can provide services at a far lower cost. We call it **outsourcing.** What do you think the advantages and risks are of going offshore?

UNIT 2. Project Management

Fill in the blanks with the correct words

- ☐ game-changer
- ☐ unveil
- ☐ emulate
- ☐ hobbled
- ☐ megatrend
- ☐ volatile
- ☐ resilience

1. to imitate; strive to equal or excel : ....
2. to be impeded or set at a disadvantage; constrained : ....
3. a trend that promises to globalize and dramatically affect the way of life : ....
4. to make public; reveal : ....
5. tending to fluctuate sharply and regularly : ....
6. The property of a material that enables it to resume its original shape or position after being bent, stretched, or compressed : ....
7. a new factor or improvement that noticeably or drastically shifts behavior, production, or other systems : ....

2. Dialogue   Practice the dialogue and answer the questions.

Just-in-Time

Enzo Hi, Jacinta. What do you think about the new production schedule?

Jacinta Well, price-matching in this brutal economy has made our profit margin razor thin.

Enzo On top of that, the markets have been so volatile. Every day sees a new swing in the stock market.

Jacinta Luckily, we've shown resilience, and our pace of innovation has kept us ahead of the trend.

Enzo Also, management was smart to invest in lean manufacturing. Now we don't have too much capital tied up.

Jacinta We're faster, too. I'm starting to love this just-in-time production! At first, it was stressing me out!

Enzo Likewise, initially I also felt hobbled by this demand because we were not quite ready for it. However, it seems to be a megatrend sweeping the globe.

Jacinta It sure is a game-changer! We should not only emulate the best practices and products, but unveil our own ideas from time to time.

Enzo With production runs becoming shorter, faster, and more complex, I feel like my mind needs to be the same way!

Jacinta Tell me about it!

A Situation
Summarize the situation in your own words.

....

B Questions

1. "Resilience" means the ability to withstand adversity and setbacks. In what ways has your company overcome obstacles to stay competitive?

2. Jacinta talks about **price-matching** and about how hard it is as a result for her company to make a hefty profit margin. What are your thoughts on price-matching? Should all companies do it? Are there any dangers?

3. Do you have a favorite **"game-changer"** from the last 10 years?

* The term "game-changer" originally comes from sports, where the introduction or absence of a factor such as a star player changes the course and expected outcome of the contest. In business, a game-changer is an element such as new technology that radically alters how business is done. For example, Wi-Fi and satellite technology have allowed the Internet to reach places where cables are absent. Thus, even people in remote places can find information easily.

3. Language Practice

Guess the meaning of each chunk and create a new sentence.

1 lean manufacturing

e.g. In the super-competitive future, lean manufacturing will make more sense and be more indispensable than ever.

:

2 sweep the globe

e.g. New ideas and technology that sweep the globe are nowadays called game-changers.

:

3 brutal economy

e.g. Our company has two essential strategies to thrive in today's brutal economy.

:

4 ahead of the trend

e.g. The company has been always a step ahead of the trend.

:

5 swings in the stock market

e.g. We have seen triple-digit swings in the stock market.

:

6 production run

e.g. There is already a waiting list with the first production run of 1,000.

:

4. Role Plays

Look at each situation and role play with your partner.

Just-in-Time (JIT) Manufacturing

Three Star Electronics recently merged with Modern Electronics, and the new Board of Directors is looking for ways to streamline its manufacturing. A Senior Vice President with Modern recently toured the manufacturing floor of Three Star and noticed large amounts of works-in-process and finished goods stacking up on the factory floor. Moreover, when he reviewed the overall manufacturing process, he was astounded by the long production times, high defect rates, delivery problems, and high costs.
He recommends switching to a JIT system and is discussing the change with the Manufacturing Manager.

Role A Senior Vice President	Role B Manufacturing Manager
Explains the benefits of a JIT system.	Expresses his concern with the cost of introducing the new system.
Expresses his belief that the long-term benefits and savings will offset the implementation costs.	Expresses further concern, specifically that a disruption in the supply chain could have drastic effects in a JIT system. Cites an example in which a fire at a brake supplier forced Toyota to shut down its assembly line, costing the company $15 billion in sales.
Appreciates his concern and praises his thoughtfulness, but assures him that the company will take the steps necessary to ensure a stable supply chain.	Tells the Senior VP that he looks forward to implementing the JIT system and requests assistance in retraining his assembly line workers.

B. Raw Material Supplier and Strategic Alliances

In this day and age, the prices of many key commodities are at all-time highs. This, combined with severe price volatility and increasingly globalized supply chains, has significantly affected manufacturing companies. One such company is Comtel, a manufacturer of computer chips. Comtel depends on securing rare earth metals from Chinese suppliers. Comtel's CEO is meeting with the CEO of one of the company's most important suppliers, Ore Tech, to discuss forming a strategic alliance so that Comtel can protect its supply chain and improve its bottom line.

Role A CEO, Comtel 	Role B CEO, Ore Tech 
Wants to agree on a long-term supply commitment. Explains that the alliance could lower costs for both companies.	Expresses his desire to receive firm and steady order commitments from Comtel so that his company can better plan production capacity.
Would like to see reductions in price volatility and to receive advance notice if price changes occur.	Suggests creating a link in information technology systems in order to streamline ordering and delivery.
Stresses the importance of an alliance for both companies. Explains that they can both be more competitive as a result.	Agrees that an alliance is mutually beneficial.

5. Business Issue & Discussion

Read the short passage and discuss the questions in as much detail as possible.

Scheduling Problems

Production scheduling tends to produce a division between the sales team and the manufacturing team, with management stuck sorting out the problems. However, management often sides with the sales team, as both endeavor to maximize profits. The manufacturing team's goal is to work steadily and produce products at a reasonable cost. Below are a few scheduling problems that can cause friction within the company.

Scheduler Can't Say No

The scheduler is aware that he cannot meet a salesman's request but cannot tell the salesman no. Or, the scheduler tells him or her no, the salesman complains to management, and management instructs the scheduler to fill the order.

Scheduling the Maximum Amount of Production Every Week

The scheduler does not schedule any downtime for rush/special orders, staff absences, equipment break downs, or other production problems. The salesmen then bear the brunt of the delayed orders.

Production Level Fluctuates Too Much

Equipment failures, staff absences, and a poor facility layout all affect production levels. Salesmen expect their manufacturing team to be capable of producing consistent amounts from week to week.

① Of the three problems, which do you feel could cause the biggest divide between the sales team, the manufacturing team, and management?

② Is management to blame for any of these problems? How can management best resolve these issues?

③ Can you think of any other problems that could occur because of improper scheduling?

6. Business Skills [Meeting Skills]

Learn the useful expressions that will emphasize your point of view and complete the task.

Persuasion

As a manager, if you are going to persuade other decision makers within the company to implement a change, it is not enough just to explain how the change will benefit the company. You need to highlight the advantages in a compelling and convincing manner.

Below are a few expressions that will emphasize your point of view, as well as a few to move on toward implementing your change.

❶ Emphasis
- "I have no doubt at all that…"
- "I am sure you will agree that…"
- "It is vital that…"
- "There has been a real need for…"
- "I would like to enumerate the advantages of…"

❷ Moving On
- "Great! Now can we move on to…?"
- "All right, now we should turn to…"
- "Let's go on to…"
- "I'm glad you agree. Shall we talk about…?"
- "You won't regret it. Now let's discuss…"

Task

In 2012, Apple implemented a new initiative that strengthened its image as an environmentally friendly, "green" company. Apple designed the packaging for its iPod headphones out of tapioca paper, which is biodegradable and dissolves in water. While Apple downplays any benefits to the company, stressing only its environmental advantages, the packaging not only appeals to environmentally conscious consumers, but also promotes Apple's strategy of innovation.

Situation: Like Apple, you would like your company to introduce some green initiatives. You will hold a meeting in which you attempt to convince upper management that these initiatives would be beneficial to your company, a bicycle manufacturer.

❶ Complete the meeting agenda below to list the initiatives, note how they will benefit the company and the environment, and explain how they will be implemented.

❷ Hold a meeting and persuade the upper management.

❸ You must be knowledgeable and persuasive when explaining the ways in which the manufacturing can "go green" by using the expressions provided above.

Agenda 1: Green Manufacturing Benefits		Agenda 2: Implementation
Green Initiative	**Benefit(s)**	**Implementation Plan**
Example: Incentive program for employees who ride their bikes to work.	Positive image for a bike company	Appoint a bike coordinator
	Reduced vehicle emissions	Find out about cycling conditions near the workplace
	Healthier workforce	Help employees plan safe routes to work

Wrapping Up! Tell four things that you learned from this lesson to review the main ideas.

1. _____ 2. _____ 3. _____ 4. _____

UNIT 2. Project Management

Lesson 07
Monitoring & Feedback

Learning Objectives

Upon completion of this lesson, you will be able to...
» discuss and learn how to give feedback
» explain problems and learn how to deal with complaints

"Feedback is the breakfast of champions."
_ Ken Blanchard

"You need to know about customer feedback that says things should be better."
_ Bill Gates

"Negative feedback is better that none. I would rather have a man hate me than overlook me. As long as he hates me I make a difference."
_ Hugh Prather

1. Warm Up Activities

A Talk about your experience.

Which of the followings is most important to consider when you give feedback to someone? Check and explain with your experience.

- [ ] Be straightforward, specific, clear, and concise.
- [ ] Make feedback timely to the event or situation.
- [ ] Discuss alternative solutions to problems.
- [ ] Give criticism in private — never in public.
- [ ] Ask open-ended questions to explore the situation.
- [ ] Listen to the other person's reason, or explanation.

B Discuss the types of feedback.

The following are types of feedback. Which type of feedback do you prefer? Think of the advantages and disadvantages of each type.

- [ ] Face-to-face feedback
- [ ] Anonymous feedback
- [ ] 360-degree feedback
- [ ] Web-based feedback
- [ ] Bottom-up feedback

Fill in the blanks with the correct words

- [ ] exude
- [ ] gravitas
- [ ] pitfall
- [ ] empathy
- [ ] buzzword
- [ ] forthright
- [ ] tackle

1. feeling conscientious toward or about by taking on the feelings and mindset of another; sharing the same feelings : ....
2. to deal with (a person) on some problem or issues : ....
3. to display abundantly : ....
4. going straight to the point; frank; direct; outspoken : ....
5. a word, often originating in a particular jargon, that becomes a vogue word in the community : ....
6. thigh seriousness; commanding respect and attention : ....
7. a hidden, and possibly catastrophic, danger : ....

2. Dialogue   Practice the dialogue and answer the questions.

Quarterly Review

Adelle You know we got the quarterly reviews this week?

Pierce Quite right! I just hope to be spared all the buzzwords and that we just cut to the chase.

Adelle I hate technospeak! Luckily, our new manager is forthright and exudes confidence.

Pierce I appreciate his gravitas, too! He looks and acts like a leader, so his comments are much easier to take.

Adelle He has gotten the entire department to invest in his ideas and become stakeholders in the company mission.

Pierce Plus, he is so good at having empathy. Naturally, I feel like we share a lot of common ground or at least I feel heard.

Adelle I totally feed off the energy in the office lately, so I don't mind all the tough love.

Pierce Before, I felt like there were so many pitfalls in dealing with management. No wonder so many employees suffered burnout.

Adelle The odds are good that everyone will feel pumped up about these meetings even if they are critical.

Pierce We can't tackle a problem if we can't identify it. So, I hope to avail myself this time around.

A Situation
Summarize the situation in your own words.

B Questions

1. A company works best when the employees truly believe in the message.
   How do companies create sincere workers? Do you know of any strategies or techniques? Which method you think is most effective in energizing the workstaff.

2. Gravitas is the weight and force of personality to command respect and attention.
   How much do you value gravitas in a leader as opposed to another quality like shrewdness or humor? How do you define "gravitas"?

3. The concept of **"feeding off the energy"** means that one person's performance, action, or attitude increases your own performance. Basically, it is like **"synergy"** where each member affects the others. Can you explain how "synergy" works in your office? In what ways have you tried to add or be aware of the "synergy" in your office?

3. Language Practice

Guess the meaning of each chunk and create a new sentence.

1 common ground

e.g. When debating contentious issues, it is best to establish some common ground.

:

2 feed off the energy

e.g. People feed off the positive energy you give them.

:

3 cut to the chase

e.g. After a few introductory comments, we cut to the chase and began negotiating.

:

4 pump up

e.g. The team leader tried to pump the team up so they would win.

:

5 avail (oneself)

e.g. Guests are encouraged to avail themselves of the full range of hotel facilities.

:

6 tackle a problem

e.g. He is trying to tackle a problem of homelessness.

:

4. Role Plays

Look at each situation and role play with your partner.

A Quality Control

The Food and Drug Administration (FDA) is investigating a popular confectionary company, Neptune Inc., because its Chocochoc candy bar may have caused a recent Salmonella outbreak. Initially, Neptune is confident in its quality control systems and details the numerous precautions currently in place to assure safe products. Yet, during the course of the meeting, the FDA inspector finds a weakness in their quality control system and suspects it may have led to the tainted food.

Role A — FDA Inspector	Role B — Quality Control Manager
Asks about any quality problems they may have had in the past. Questions Neptune's commitment to quality control.	Admits to a few minor problems that they had years ago, but then details the rigorous quality control standards that they have since put in place.
Requests an overview of their manufacturing procedures, in-process analyses, cleaning and sanitizing programs, product standards, etc.	Reviews the company's procedures with the inspector.
Notices that they do not have any procedures for monitoring raw materials and suspects that the problem may have started with one of Neptune's suppliers.	Acknowledges the gap in quality control. Suggests a way to strengthen their procedures. Discusses their recall procedures.

Lesson 07 / Monitoring & Feedback

B. Outsource Monitoring

Athena, a European shoe outfitter, has decided to outsource its manufacturing to a company in Bangladesh so that it can focus its attention on marketing and advertising. However, one of the managers within Athena is concerned that the company might acquire a poor reputation because she has heard about the poor conditions that exist in many Bangladesh manufacturing companies.

The manager even cites a fire at one of the factories in which more than a hundred workers died. She approaches one of the other managers who fully supported outsourcing to Bangladesh.

Role A — Concerned Manager	Role B — Pro-Outsourcing Manager
Expresses her concern about outsourcing to Bangladesh and the potential long-term effects it could have on the company.	Details the standards and "Code of Conduct" that the Bangladesh manufacturer will have to follow.
Asks about the monitoring systems that are being put in place.	Discusses the ways in which Athena will monitor the factory like live video feeds and surprise inspections.
Suggests additional methods of monitoring such as placing a full-time independent monitoring team with the factory.	Talks about the concerned manager's suggestions and assures her that everything will be done to protect the workers and Athena.

5. Business Issue & Discussion

Read the short passage and discuss the questions in as much detail as possible.

Financial vs. Non-financial Performance Measures

The purpose of a performance monitoring and measurement system should be to help the organization achieve its strategic goals. With this in mind, should a performance measurement system center on financial or non-financial indicators? Consider the following views.

> "When you can measure what you are speaking about and express it in numbers, you know something about it."

> "Not everything that counts can be counted, and not everything that can be counted counts."

Many of the managers in today's business world would side with the first view and are trained to believe that financial outcomes provide the simplest and most appropriate way to demonstrate growth and roductivity. However, naysayers point out that this approach encourages short-term thinking, decisions that are misaligned to the organization's mission, and in the worst-case, fraud. As supported by the second view, performance must also be judged on factors such as quality, customer satisfaction, and innovation.

1. Do you feel that financial or non-financial measures are better methods of evaluating employees? Why?

2. Discuss some other types of non-financial measures that can be used to gauge performance.

3. Are there any disadvantages to using non-financial measures? Is there a way to integrate both financial and non-financial measures?

UNIT 2. Project Management

6. Business Skills [Business Writing Skills]

Read the following short passage about "Electronic Memo & Purpose Statement" and complete the task. Use the useful expressions provided while you do the task.

Electronic Memo & Purpose Statement

These days, a significant portion of inter-company correspondence takes place via e-mail, and even formal memos are going from paper to wire. When composing an electronic memo, one of the first things you must do is to notify the recipient of the subject of your communication. This is often called the purpose statement. Here are a few suggestions.

- "I am writing to let you know that..."
- "The reason that I am writing is..."
- "Please be aware/informed that..."
- "The purpose of this e-mail is..."

Task

Situation: You are a Senior Manager for Titan Construction. Your firm has just been awarded the contract for the new Alphaville Ants baseball stadium. It will be your job to oversee the Project Manager. Before the project gets underway, you write him an e-mail outlining the procedures that you expect him to follow during the course of construction, including what should be monitored, how often, and what records should be kept.

1. Complete a monitoring chart below that includes at least five monitoring procedures (the first one has been done for you).

2. Write an e-mail to your Project Manager.

3. Be sure to start your note with a purpose statement.

Project Management Monitoring Checklist

Category	Procedure(s)	Frequency	Required Records
Noise	Measure sound levels at the property line	Daily	Noise Log
	Submit a plan for anything over 80 dB	As needed	Excess Noise Plan
	Restrict activity in excess of 80 dB from 10am to 4pm	As needed	None
	Inspect noise barriers	Weekly	Inspection Log

Wrapping Up! Tell four things that you learned from this lesson to review the main ideas.

1. _____   2. _____   3. _____   4. _____

UNIT 2. Project Management

Lesson 08
Risk Management

Learning Objectives

Upon completion of this lesson, you will be able to...
» discuss everyday risk and uncertainty in business
» talk about alternative options and make the best business decision

"A good rule of thumb is to assume that everything matters."
_ Richard Thaler

"When solving problems, dig at the roots instead of just hacking at the leaves."
_ Anthony J. D'Angelo

"When you find yourself in a hole, stop digging."
_ Will Rogers

1. Warm Up Activities

A Talk about "cyber risk"

These days, the Internet is the great enabler of commerce and communication. However, this wondrous network also carries the potential to harm. Listed below are some potential harms from the Internet. Rank each of them and explain how you or your company would deal with each one.

- [ ] False information or lies about your company.
- [ ] ID theft; Stealing your customers' information.
- [ ] Shutting down your website.
- [ ] Mimicking your company name and service to create confusion among customers.
- [ ] Spying and stealing trade secrets.
- [ ] Spam with malware that could ruin your computer and operating system.

B Discuss the following questions:

1 *Hedging* can mean to take an action that limits the negative consequences of another action or enterprise. In simple language, a hedge is used to reduce any substantial losses/gains suffered by an individual or an organization. Give an example from your life where you made a decision to protect against possible loss.

2 *Blind spots* are troubled areas or hidden problems that can hurt us but which by nature we cannot easily identify or choose to ignore. Could you name some possible blind spots in your company, institute, nation, etc? Which areas do you think might be blind spots (i.e. areas of weakness not being fully dealt with currently)?

UNIT 2. Project Management

fill in the blanks with the correct words

- ☐ catastrophe
- ☐ foreseeable
- ☐ agile
- ☐ fallout
- ☐ toxic
- ☐ avert
- ☐ aftermath
- ☐ dilemma
- ☐ paralysis

1. a sudden and widespread disaster : ....
2. an unexpected or incidental effect, outcome, or product : ....
3. quickly resourceful; easily adaptable; being fast and responsive : ....
4. something that results or follows from an event, especially one of a disastrous or unfortunate nature : ....
5. poisonous; (financial) so worthless to be ruinous : ....
6. to ward off; turn away or aside; blunt : ....
7. a situation that requires a choice between options that are or seem to be equally unfavorable or mutually exclusive : ....
8. capable of being anticipated : ....
9. the state of being unable to move, act or function properly : ....

2. Dialogue   Practice the dialogue and answer the questions.

Hedging Bets

Leah   Ugh! Did you see today's headline and stock index in the *Financial News?* The forecast is for anemic demand, and our sector looks all but moribund for the foreseeable future.

Morgan   It's wretched. All these blind spots lurking in the economy were really of our own devising. A bit more due diligence—you know, fact checking and asking the hard questions—would have spared us all this trouble.

Leah   I think it is about time that every company appoints a CRO, a Chief Risk Officer. You can't be too sure of anything these days!

Morgan   Right! With more expertise, we could simulate the possible consequences of our ventures.

Leah   Yep, being able to winnow out the toxic options is a big part of handling dilemmas and averting catastrophes.

Morgan   The aftermath of this crisis has yet to be seen it its full scope. We should be agile to respond to further fallout.

Leah   To make matters worse, I fear trade embargoes could disrupt trade and balance sheets across the board, not to mention the national budget.

Morgan   Well, action is almost always better than inaction, so really I fear too much paralysis on our part. I want to stay nimble. Like Steve Jobs said, "Stay Hungry. Stay Foolish."

A   Situation
Summarize the situation in your own words.
....
....

B   Questions

1. What does Leah think that the company should do to manage risk? Is it a good idea?
2. What does Morgan think are some of the causes of the current economic problems?
3. What are some of Leah's tactics for avoiding bad decisions?
4. An increasingly popular job title is CRO : Chief Risk Officer. Think of the function and purpose of this job in your particular company and industry. List three specific functions for these persons to fulfill.
5. What do you think about the adage: **"Action is better than inaction"**? Do you think that being "on the move" is always better than just keeping things steady? Identify any factors than increase or suppress your risk appetite.

3. Language Practice

Guess the meaning of each chunk and create a new sentence.

1 winnow out

e.g. To make a wise choice, it is best to start broad and winnow out the inferior options.

:

2 anemic demand

e.g. A weak economy is characterized by anemic demand, among other factors.

:

3 trade embargoes

e.g. Political disputes or accusations of unfair practices like higher than normal import tariffs can result in trade embargoes.

:

4 due diligence

e.g. Before buying out a competitor, due diligence is a necessary step in evaluating worth.

:

5 blind spots

e.g. Does your business have a blind spot that is hurting your sales and growth?

:

6 full scope

e.g. We have to really begin with the full scope safeguard agreements.

:

4. Role Plays

Look at each situation and role play with your partner.

A Managing the Risk of Rising Fuel Costs

International Parcel Service (IPS) is a global package delivery company that maintains a large fleet of airplanes and trucks. Accordingly, one of the company's biggest costs is fuel. Experts anticipate that conflicts in the Middle East will lead to higher fuel costs, and the CEO of IPS would like his VP of Operations to formulate a risk management strategy that insulates IPS against rising fuel costs and allows them to avert financial disaster.

 **Role A — CEO**   **Role B — VP of Operations**

Role A — CEO	Role B — VP of Operations
Asks the VP to outline his risk management strategies.	Believes that the company should: a) invest in hybrids; b) reorganize the fleet and match the most cost-effective vehicle to each delivery; c) redraw delivery routes to minimize distances; and d) install smaller engines in some of the vehicles.
Requests that the VP address their fleet of airplanes.	Informs him that his team has found ways to decrease the weights of the planes.
Asks the VP if he has considered a hedging strategy, citing the successes of Southwest Airlines.	Tells the CEO that he has discussed a hedging strategy with the Finance Department and that they are formalizing a plan.

B. Competition Risk

A major facet of risk management is analyzing the ways in which your company could lose market share due to changes in the market and/or from the actions of competitors. Two managers for Donut Domain, a popular donut and coffee chain, are now discussing their company's competition risk.

 Role A Manager A	Role B Manager B
Discusses their direct and indirect competitors and the potential impacts to Donut Domain.	Raises the point that Starbucks will soon start offering donuts and that another donut chain, Holy Donut, will be introducing a new line of "healthy donuts."
Talks about the state of the donut market and the continued reports about the negative health effects of donuts.	Believes that they need to differentiate their products and branch out beyond donuts (e.g. sandwiches).
Explains ways in which they can defend their position through Donut Domains brand strategy such as emphasizing the quality of the company's coffee.	Suggests forming a strategic alliance with select grocery stores to gain a competitive edge on the competitors.

5. Business Issue & Discussion

Read the short passage and discuss the questions in as much detail as possible.

Risk Management: Adversary or Partner to Innovation

There is a view that risk management policies crush the entrepreneurial spirit within a company, discouraging managers from thinking outside the box. Uncertainty is inherent to innovation, and some believe that risk management and innovation can never go hand-in-hand. However, good risk management is not about completely evading risk any more than good innovation is about trying to be new without considering the consequences. In fact, risk management and innovation can be partners, not adversaries. If done properly, effective risk management can reveal areas of underinvestment and expose new opportunities that may otherwise have been ignored. Risk management should not be viewed as a safety procedure but as a learning process.

1. Do you feel that risk management and innovation can coexist? Or, do risk management policies indeed hamper innovation?

2. How can trying to eliminate risks from a company actually stimulate innovation? Can you think of any specific examples?

3. Which do you think is more important—to mitigate risk or to be innovative? Does it depend on the type and size of the organization?

Lesson 08 / Risk Management   51

6. Business Skills [Presentation Skills]

Read the following short passage about "Risk Management" and complete the task. Use the useful expressions provided while you do the task.

Risk Management

In general, risk management is based on four steps: risk identification, risk analysis, risk treatment, and monitoring of risks.

1 Risk Identification
- Identification of risks and their causes

2 Risk Analysis / Assessment
- Estimation of likelihood and impact of risks
- Quantitative vs. Qualitative

3 Risk Treatment
- Actions and mechanisms to minimize risks
- Risk acceptance

4 Monitoring & Review

Task

Situation: Biltmore Hotels is holding its annual conference to discuss new corporate policies, financial performance, strategy, etc. The Risk Manager will lead a seminar in the morning on risk management and your team has to meet in groups the night before and discuss the risk management chart.

1 Participate in a meeting with your co-workers and discuss the types of risks that exist in your industry.

2 Carry those risks through the risk management process, estimating their likelihood, finding mechanisms to reduce them, and so on. Then, fill in the blanks below.

- Topic : _____

1. Risk Identification : _____
2. Risk Analysis/ Assessment : _____
3. Risk Treatment : _____
4. Monitoring & Review : _____

3 Decisions are often made in a group setting, so if you want to be successful in this environment, you must speak up and deliver your ideas to the group. The useful expressions will allow you to express more eloquently your opinion, disagreement, or confusion.

4 The Risk Manager will lead off his presentation with a discussion of the chart.

USEFUL EXPRESSIONS

1. When you agree:
- "Did anyone mention...?"
- "Another opinion we may want to consider..."

2. When you disagree:
- "My experience has actually been quite different..."
- "I just want to play devil's advocate here for a moment, but what if we were to...?"

3. When you are confused:
- "I'm not entirely sure I'm following you. Could you...?"
- "This may be a dumb question, but..."

Wrapping Up!
Tell four things that you learned from this lesson to review the main ideas.

1. _____   2. _____   3. _____   4. _____

02 Moving Ahead during Turbulent Times

> The CEO sets up four principles in order to maintain the company's stability throughout the global financial crisis.

⦿ Background

DuPont was founded in 1802 as a gunpowder mill and has grown to become the world's third largest chemical company with $28 billion in revenues and $1.8 billion in profits. The company employs 70,000 people worldwide.

⦿ A Looming Financial Crisis

The impact of the financial crisis began to hit DuPont in September 2008. Sales volume slid, good customers cancelled orders, and employees were gripped by fear and uncertainty. As the environment worsened and sales fell by up to 50% in some units, DuPont CEO Ellen J. Kullman ordered two traumatic restructurings. Perhaps more importantly for DuPont's future, Kullman also concluded that the company faced a "new reality" requiring fundamental changes if it were to remain successful.

⦿ Managing Crisis

In times of financial crisis, what strategies would you employ to weather the storm?

Add your own ideas to the list; then, choose the best three strategies. Discuss your ideas with your team members.

- ☐ Layoff employees
- ☐ Cut back senior management salaries
- ☐ Stop all unnecessary spending
- ☐ Cancel all executive travel
- ☐ Sell off assets
- ☐ Take out bank loans
- ☐ Seek new and different markets
- ☐ Develop new products
- ☐ Renegotiate prices with clients (up or down)
- ☐ Close offices in foreign countries
- ☐ Issue more shares to raise capital
- ☐ Seek ideas from employees through "town hall" meetings
- ☐ Set up an "idea brainstorm" page on the company intranet
- ☐ Cancel all employee benefits and holidays
- ☐ Look for a partner who could merge to form a more synergistic business concept

Add your own ideas:

* ....
* ....
* ....

CASE STUDY 02

◉ Kullman's Leadership Principles

CEO Ellen Kullman's used the following four principles to guide DuPont through financial crisis:

Principle 1 — Focus on what you can control. DuPont found new markets for existing products, like selling products designed for India's railways to China.

Principle 2 — Adopt a new trajectory by rethinking your business model. Get people to think differently about a business model that had always measured success based on plant capacity. DuPont developed service-based products to re-engage customers.

Principle 3 — Communication is key. Kullman saw the need to develop an aligned team that clearly understood the company's goals and tradeoffs.

Principle 4 — Maintain the company's mission, which is "sustainable growth," by increasing shareholder value and reducing DuPont's environmental footprint. Kullman maintained that if you capture the heart and soul, you will be successful.

◉ Analyze

Q1) What is your opinion of Kullman's four principles?
Q2) Why is it important for senior managers to be able to communicate effectively with their employees?
Q3) Whose responsibility is it to deal with a financial crisis at a company?
Q4) Why should companies be concerned with environmental issues even in times of economic downturn?
Q5) What is the importance of diversification at a company, especially during a downturn?

◉ Presentation

Make a presentation based on the following:
Your company faces a major downturn because of the global economic crisis. You need a plan of action to manage the company, and you decide to adopt Kullman's four principles model. You must reassure your employees and unveil a strategy to boost morale and give new direction to the company. Use whatever resources are available to make the necessary transitions.

Principle 1. New markets for existing products	....
Principle 2. Your new business model	....
Principle 3. Ways to communicate effectively	....
Principle 4. Your company's mission	....

UNIT 3. Business Strategy

Lesson 09
Strategic Planning

Learning Objectives

Upon completion of this lesson, you will be able to...
» explain future plans and share the vision and mission of a company
» discuss how to increase business flexibility

"Different isn't always better, but better is always different."
_ Dale Dauten

"If you don't know the Jewelry, know the Jeweller"
_ Warren Buffett

"Great ideas need landing gear as well as wings."
_ C.D. Jackson

1. Warm Up Activities

A Big Picture + Tactics

Roger Martin, Dean of the Rottman School of Management at Toronto University, suggests that to make strategic planning easier, you should first just tell a happy story. That way you identify a goal that is worthy. Then you fill in the process from the current day to the eventual goal with concrete steps along the way.

- Tell a happy story about your company three to five years from now?
- Explain 1-3 steps that would get you to that goal?

B Future Uncertainty

The future is always uncertain no matter what plans we make. Thus, strategic planning is not a way to control the future but a way to measure performance against a logical goal as the future unfolds.

- Talk about one way that you measure your own performance on a daily basis?
- Discuss how your company measures performance on a weekly, monthly, or yearly basis?

C Idea Generator and Business Flexibility

To promote the free exchange of ideas, some companies create "idea rooms" where all the workers are equal. In these spaces, every worker temporarily abandons his or her rank, i.e. leaves his or her title at the door.

- What is your reaction to such an idea?
- Would you want to spend time in an idea room where you can freely criticize and offer ideas?
- Do you think it is possible for workers really to treat each other as if titles did not exist?

Fill in the blanks with the correct words

- [ ] formulate
- [ ] savvy
- [ ] pre-emptive
- [ ] downside
- [ ] infringe
- [ ] murky
- [ ] obsolete

1. no longer in use or no longer useful : ....
2. to develop a plan, system, or proposal carefully, thinking about all details : ....
3. vague or obscure; hard to see or define : ....
4. aving quick perception, comprehension, and/or ability : ....
5. negative aspect; negative trend : ....
6. to violate the law or the rights or property of another; overstep a boundary : ....
7. taking initiative; doing something first : ....

2. Dialogue Practice the dialogue and answer the questions.

Drill Down & Scale-Up

Aurora Okay, so first of all, our brand is known for its savvy image. So, we should promote that foremost.

Caiden Yes, and secondly, we should drill down on the data that our marketing team has already.

Aurora For sure. Once we know local preferences for flavors, colors, and textures, then we can start to scale-up operations.

Caiden How to enter a market can seem so murky at first! So, I am glad that we captured some data and have formulated a plan.

Aurora As always, our image should be welcoming to all, but it is key to keep in mind our core customer.

Caiden Then we can establish some price points that will create customer spending.

Aurora Well, it looks like it was advantageous to be so pre-emptive in entering this market. Although the coffee-cafe culture is a bit new here, there seem to be signs of acceptance.

Caiden So far I cannot see any downside, but it might take awhile for consumer demand to pick up.

Aurora Well, at the first sustained rise in demand, I will perk-up for sure!

A Situation
Summarize the situation in your own words.

B Questions

1. Aurora talks about her company's savvy image. How would you describe your company's image? Has it changed at all over the years through marketing and re-positioning? If you could add one more word or value, which word would you add?

2. Being pre-emptive could carry a big reward but it could be risky. Could you explain the potential risk and the potential reward of being pre-emptive?

3. Caiden comments that the future is usually murky but a plan helps. Could you discuss a time when a plan gave you or your team a reason and way to act? Did the plan later change? If so, how was it good or bad to have a first plan initially as opposed to no plan?

3. Language Practice

Guess the meaning of each chunk and create a new sentence.

1 drill down on the data
e.g. First, we need to collect data from our customers. Then to assess its value, we need to drill down on the data to find future sales opportunities.
:

2 scale-up operations
e.g. To reach more customers and create a bigger brand presence than our competitors, we should consider whether to scale-up operations.
:

3 core customer
e.g. Whenever our company makes a decision, we always think foremost about how it will affect our core customer.
:

4 price points
e.g. To maximize profits, we create a graph to show how different price points would affect sales.
:

5 local preference
e.g. Local preference and tradition must be taken into consideration.
:

6 enter a market
e.g. There are a variety of ways to enter an overseas market.
:

4. Role Plays

Look at each situation and role play with your partner.

A Implementing Strategy

The strategic planning process is exactly that--a process. Formulating strategy does not guarantee that the desired performance will be reached any more than having a roadmap guarantees that a driver will reach his destination. It seems obvious, yet most companies create plans that never get put into practice. HealthSouth Hospitals lost 10% of its market share to its largest competitor last year, and the CEO is blaming that on poor implementation. So, he is discussing ways to remedy it with his Vice President.

Role A — CEO
- Believes that the strategic plan was not effectively communicated to the employees.
- Stresses keeping the employees focused on the long-term goals and not just the day-to-day activities.
- Suggests linking the strategy to incentives that reward those who successfully achieve the goals.

Role B — Vice President
- Points out that while strategy was discussed at last year's annual meeting, implementation was not.
- Recommends assigning an "owner" to each objective so that someone is accountable for its success or failure.
- Proposes additional training opportunities so that the employees have the skills to support the plan.

B Strategic Planning – Supply Chain

GL, Inc. is a growing appliance company. GL's business strategy is shifting toward being the low-cost provider in the industry. The supply chain strategy should support the business strategy, so the Vice President of Manufacturing is talking to one of his Managers about driving down the costs in their supply chain.

Role A — VP, Manufacturing

- Suggests focusing on the Chinese market because they gain more supply chain efficiencies there.
- Discusses shipping alternatives so that they can lower their shipping costs.
- Discusses outsourcing some of their functions in an attempt to reduce costs.

Role B — Manager

- Suggests examining their overhead costs and replacing old machinery, which have high operational costs.
- Discusses buying key suppliers, forming joint ventures, strategic alliances, etc.
- Agrees with outsourcing so that the company can focus on its key competencies.

5. Business Issue & Discussion

Read the short passage and discuss the questions in as much detail as possible.

The Balanced Scorecard

The Balanced Scorecard (BSC) is a strategic planning and management tool that aligns business activities to the organization's strategy by combining non-financial measures with traditional financial metrics. In essence, it attempts to translate a firm's vague, intangible vision into specific, measurable goals. A balanced scorecard for a refrigerator manufacturer is provided as an example.

Because of the BSC's ability to capture both financial goals and key non-financial drivers, its use is widespread. However, critics argue that the BSC is not without weaknesses.

1. The BSC requires significant time and effort to formulate clearly stated objectives in each of the four areas. Moreover, implementation requires complete organizational collaboration.
2. The four areas presented in the BSC do not paint a complete picture. The financial information included on the scorecard is limited.
3. Many organizations use metrics that do not fit their business.
4. The Balanced Scorecard excludes suppliers, the environment, and competitors.

① Do you think that all of the listed weaknesses result from the actual design of the Balanced Scorecard?

② Is the Balanced Scorecard adequate on its own, or does it need to be part of a bigger strategy?

③ How could the Balanced Scorecard be modified to include suppliers, the environment, and/or competitors?

BALANCED SCORECARD - POLAR REFRIGERATORS

	OBJECTIVE	MEASURE	TARGET	INITIATIVE
FINANCIAL	Decrease Energy Consumption	Energy Cost / Output	20% Decrease	• Establish Energy Shut-down Procedures • Replace Factory Lights
CUSTOMER	Industry-Leading Customer Loyalty	Customer Satisfaction Rating	80% Satisfaction Rating	• Customer Loyalty Program • Mystery Shopper Program
INTERNAL BUSINESS PROCESSES	Reduced Defective Output	% Defective Output	4% to 2% Defective Rate	• Employee Training Program • Investment in New Machinery
LEARNING & GROWTH	Increase Employee Retention	% of Key Staff Turnover	20% to 15% Turnover Rate	• Employee Loyalty Program • Employee Stock Option Plan

VISION & STRATEGY

6. Business Skills [Meeting Skills]

Read the following short passage about "Good or Bad Vision and Mission Statement" and complete the task. Use the useful expressions provided while you do the task.

Debate: Good or Bad Vision and Mission Statements

If a leader's goal is to build a collaborative and transparent culture with his or her organization, the leader should welcome vigorous debates and assemble a team who will challenge each other and fight for their ideas and beliefs. Should you work in this type of organization, you will find yourself in the middle of many heated discussions. Debating requires a particular set of skills and phrases.

Task

Look over the following vision and mission statements. Then, participate in a debate that ultimately builds a consensus as to whether each statement is good or bad.

A Vision Statements

Microsoft
"There will be a personal computer on every desk running Microsoft software."

General Motors
"GM's vision is to be the world leader in transportation products and related services. We will earn our customers' enthusiasm through continuous improvement driven by the integrity, teamwork, and innovation of GM people."

Caterpillar
"Be the global leader in customer value."

Nike (1960)
"Crush Adidas."

B Mission Statements

Wal-Mart
"Our mission is to enhance and integrate our supplier diversity programs into all of our procurement practices and to be an advocate for minority and women-owned businesses."

Starbucks
"To inspire and nurture the human spirit—one person, one cup, one neighborhood at a time."

General Motors
"GM is a multinational corporation engaged in socially responsible operations, worldwide. It is dedicated to provide products and services of such quality that our customers will receive superior value while our employees and business partners will share our success and our stockholders will receive a sustained superior return on their investment."

USEFUL EXPRESSIONS

1 Stating an Opinion
- "If you want my honest opinion…"
- "As far as I'm concerned…"

2 Asking for an Opinion
- "Do you have anything to say about this?"
- "What are your thoughts on all of this?"

3 Expressing Agreement
- "I agree with you 100 percent."
- "I'm afraid I agree with…"

4 Expressing Disagreement
- "That's not always the case."
- "I beg to differ."

5 Interruptions
- "Is it okay if I jump in for a second?"
- (after being interrupted) "You didn't let me finish."

6 Settling an Argument
- "Let's just move on, shall we?"
- "I think we're going to have to agree to disagree."

Tell four things that you learned from this lesson to review the main ideas.

1. ....
2. ....
3. ....
4. ....

UNIT 3. Business Strategy

Lesson 10
Strategic Analysis

Learning Objectives

Upon completion of this lesson, you will be able to...
» discuss the weakness and strength of a company in the global market
» explain opportunities and threats to extending a business

"Successful business strategy is about actively shaping the game you play, not just playing the game you find."
_ Adam Brandenburger & Barry Nalebuff

"If you know the enemy and know yourself, you need not fear the results of a hundred battles. If you know yourself but not the enemy, for every victory gained you will also suffer a defeat. If you know neither the enemy nor yourself, you will succumb in every battle."
_ Sun Tsu

1. Warm Up Activities

A Discuss the following questions.

In order to judge performance it is crucial to not only judge sales but also to collect **information about customers** so that you can keep selling successfully and keep building new products that have relevance.

> **Q1.** In your market or industry, what data are you collecting about your customers?
>
> **Q2.** In what way is your data collection better than that of your competitors?
>
> **Q3.** Has your company made any decisions based on customer data?
>
> **Q4.** Do you see any room for improvement?

B Using acronyms as building tools

To analyze a performance and build a plan, companies use the framework called **SWOT: Strengths, Weaknesses, Opportunities, and Threats.** Each letter stands for an item which should be analyzed. To put this acronym into action, some companies use another acronym: USED. Talk about USED of your company with your partner.

❶ Strengths **Used** : _____

❷ Weaknesses **Stopped** : _____

❸ Opportunity **Exploited** : _____

❹ Threats **Defended Against** : _____

UNIT 3. Business Strategy

Fill in the blanks with the correct words

- [ ] validate
- [ ] template
- [ ] hone
- [ ] modify
- [ ] simulate
- [ ] prediction
- [ ] out-of-touch
- [ ] crucial

1. a mold, pattern, or outline that serves as a basis : ....
2. a statement about what you think will happen in the future : ....
3. to make more effective, intense, or sharp/accurate : ....
4. to make changes and adjustments : ....
5. no longer have recent knowledge or information about something : ....
6. to make a model of : ....
7. to support or confirm the truth or value of something : ....
8. extremely important because it has a major effect on the result of something : ....

2. Dialogue   Practice the dialogue and answer the questions.

Articulate a Strategy

Jasmine You know, these days we just seem to go around in circles with our strategies.

Bryn I think we need a new template that combines a data-driven strategy with a unique vision.

Jasmine First, we should start with a strong kick-off meeting to get new ideas and outline the basics. Then we shouldn't be afraid to hone and modify the strategy along the way.

Bryn Sure, up-to-date feedback and responses are crucial. We never want to be out-of-touch with the market, but we also want to be ahead of the curve.

Jasmine Well, ideally, we want to create the curve, but that would take some ambitious moves. So, before we get too deeply involved in any project, we should run a few pilot programs.

Bryn Great idea. Then we could simulate those markets to forecast and make some predictions.

Jasmine Exactly, once we know what we are handling, then we can validate some decisions.

Bryn Great, sounds like we need the perfect combination of aspirational thinking set against core concrete goals.

Jasmine Yep, you might call it: Hope & Realism.

Bryn Hmm. . . that could be our internal tag for this next campaign! Good word choice!

A Situation
Summarize the situation in your own words.
....
....

B Questions

1. Jasmine emphasizes how a strong "kick-off" meeting can set the tone for new developments within a company. How does your company start the planning for new endeavors? If the endeavor is to reach more customers, what is the first phase of bringing such an endeavor to the customers' attention?

2. To what extent do you think companies lead a market by creating and testing ideas? In contrast, do you think customers' desires, cultural trends, and other factors such as legislation create new needs that companies eventually discover but are not the cause of?

3. Why does Jasmine suggest pilot programs? Do you have any experience with running such a test? If you could design one for your company, what would you like to test?

3. Language Practice

Guess the meaning of each chunk and create a new sentence.

1 go around in circles

e.g. I need some more data to work on; otherwise, I'm just going around in circles.

:

2 kick-off meeting

e.g. The kick-off meeting involved both strengthening team ties and brainstorming new goals and actions for the next three to five years.

:

3 data-driven strategy

e.g. Another name for a data-driven strategy is analytics and number-crunching.

:

4 ahead of the curve

e.g. To be a market leader, you must make it your goal to be ahead of the curve.

:

5 run a pilot program

e.g. We've been running a pilot program for the last couple of years.

:

6 articulate a strategy

e.g. One of the main functions of a CEO is to articulate a strategy for the entire company.

:

4. Role Plays

Look at each situation and role play with your partner.

A. Competitive Analysis

In sports, for a team to be successful, it is necessary to understand an opponent's strengths and weaknesses before attempting to formulate a winning game plan. For example, a baseball coach will study opposing batters' tendencies and then position his fielders accordingly.

Business is no different. Failing to understand the competitive environment will put an organization on the fast track to failure. Performing a competitive analysis is essential to determine the strengths and weaknesses of the competitors within the market, strategies that will provide the company with a distinct advantage, and the barriers that can be developed in order to prevent competition from entering the market.

You and a partner are drafting a plan for a tea cafe.
Do a competitive analysis that examines your competitive environment.

Role A — Partner 1	Role B — Partner 2
Lists direct and indirect competitors and how they provide service (tea cafes, coffee shops, etc.).	Lists competitors' strengths and weaknesses and discusses how the business compares.
Sees a gap in the market. Talks about how the business will position itself.	Talks about how they can differentiate their products from those that competitors offer.
Discusses other advantages that the business has.	Discusses barriers that can be erected to prevent the entrance of other competitors.

B. Brand Analysis

An essential part of an organization's strategic planning process is branding. An effective brand strategy can provide an edge over the competition. Branding is basically the company's promise to the customer. It tells them what to expect from your products or services and distinguishes you from your competitors. A brand tells a story about the company and what it hopes to be. Thus, branding strategy cannot be conceived in a vacuum and must fit in to the company's overall strategic plan.

A skin care company is formulating a brand strategy for its new line of gentle, all natural, herbal soaps, which are developed without animal testing. Two members of the marketing team are discussing brand strategy with the aid of the visual shown below.

Role A	Marketing Team Member 1	Role B	Marketing Team Member 2
Attempts to answer the questions posed by the visual and define their target customer.		Discusses how the new product line fits into the company's overall strategy.	
Decides which of the soaps' qualities will be most important to the brand strategy and how to position the product.		Talks about the message that should be delivered and how that message will affect the name, logo, and tagline.	
Chooses the most effective marketing strategies.		Discusses how to implement and test their bran strategy.	

The Brand Drivers
- EMOTION: Does your brand connect with your customers on an emotional level?
- VALUE: Does your brand deliver the value expected?
- AWARENESS: Are your customers and key stakeholders aware of your brand?
- DIFFERENCE: Does your brand give your customers a reason to believe?

5. Business Issue & Discussion

Read the short passage and discuss the questions in as much detail as possible.

Kodak

The demise of Kodak epitomizes a company that failed to adequately plan for the future. When Kodak arrived on the scene, it changed the world of photography. However, as photography moved away from traditional film, Kodak didn't take the time to fully understand how the world of photography was changing around them. While Kodak acknowledged that digital photography could disrupt their business, top management never embraced digital and did not prepare for the digital revolution. Kodak spent its time using digital to improve its film instead of developing a true digital camera. Thus, once the age of digital cameras arrived, it was too late for Kodak to recapture its position at the top.

1. How could things have gone differently for Kodak? Why do you think top management never recognized what digital technology could do to its business?

2. How far into the future should a company look? When should a company start planning for a future change?

3. What does Kodak's story teach us about strategic planning? What does it say about a company's competitive landscape?

Lesson 10 / Strategic Analysis

6. Business Skills [Business Writing Skills]

Learn some of the consulting expressions and complete the task.

SWOT Analysis

Consulting Expressions

When a company doesn't have the in-house capabilities for a specific task, not enough resources for the task, or desires an objective view, it will often engage the services of a consultant. However, consultants seem to have their own language, and it is important to understand the expressions they use in their reports. Look at the following expressions and meanings.

Expressions	Meanings
5,000 mile view	a high, level summary view of the situation
At the end of the day	an attempt to summarize and close the discussion
B2B / B2C	business to business / business to customer
Buy-in	agreement
Circle back	to follow up at a later time
Due diligence	comprehensive study
Leverage	use
Low-hanging fruit	the initial opportunities
Opportunity cost	the cost of giving up one option for another
Pushback	resistance

Task

Situation: OoYoo, a mid-size dairy company (2,000 employees) located in northern Japan, hires the Sendai Consulting Agency to perform a SWOT Analysis. You are the consultant assigned to the project and will need to report back to the dairy company.

1. Hold a meeting with your co-workers and think of all the aspects that could come up for the company: Strengths, Weakness, Opportunities, and Threats.
2. Write a report that answers the questions in the chart below.
3. Try to use some of the consulting expressions provided above.

Strengths: S
- What is it that OoYoo does especially well?
- What resources does OoYoo have?
- What makes OoYoo unique?
- How do others view OoYoo's strengths?

Weaknesses: W
- What in OoYoo needs improvement?
- What do others perceive as OoYoo's weaknesses?
- What problems does OoYoo have with resources (components, people, assets, etc.)?

Opportunities: O
- Which of OoYoo's strengths could be used as opportunities?
- Are there new opportunities OoYoo can take advantage of?
- Are there any new trends in the market that could be beneficial to OoYoo?

Threats: T
- What threats exist in the market?
- How strong is OoYoo's competition?
- Which of OoYoo's weaknesses could turn into threats?

 **Wrapping Up!** Tell four things that you learned from this lesson to review the main ideas.

1. _____   2. _____   3. _____   4. _____

UNIT 3. Business Strategy

Lesson 11

International Commerce

Learning Objectives

Upon completion of this lesson, you will be able to...
» clarify the gap between two parties and make adjustments
» discuss contract conditions, bargain, and learn how to reach an agreement

"In business, you don't get what you deserve. You get what you negotiate."
_ Chester L. Karrass

"He who has learned to disagree without being disagreeable has discovered the most valuable secret of a diplomat."
_ Robert Estabrook

"A friendship founded on business is a good deal better than a business founded on friendship."
_ John D. Rockefeller

1. Warm Up Activities

A Discuss the following questions.

Nowadays, a popular concept in business is the idea of **"businesses without borders"**, which means doing business and being present in as many countries as possible. How do you feel about this practice: Is it beneficial to the typical worker or does it favor only the powerful? Could you list some advantages and disadvantages of the practice?

B Key factors to succeed in international commerce

Which of the following is the most significant factor to succeed international commerce?

☐ Quality of product and service
☐ Competitive price
☐ Marketing strategies
☐ Good industrial relations
☐ Knowledge about international law
☐ Cultural difference awareness
☐ Negotiation skills
☐ Sensitivity to the world economy

Lesson 11 / International Commerce

Fill in the blanks with the correct words

- ☐ hazard
- ☐ intuitive
- ☐ enhance
- ☐ backlash
- ☐ turbulence
- ☐ sluggish
- ☐ downsize

1. a strong negative or contrary reaction : ....
2. to increase or improve the value, quality, desirability, or attractiveness : ....
3. a source of danger; chance, risk : ....
4. to reduce the number of employees in a company : ....
5. sudden violent movements; many changes and disruptions : ....
6. readily learned or understood : ....
7. not moving as quickly as usual : ....

2. Dialogue Practice the dialogue and answer the questions.

Fast Mover

Ruby Well, you know, even though sales are sluggish now, I think that we could enhance our product line by teaming up with a foreign producer.

Acton That seems right. So much turbulence in the market has slowed sales, but the new trade agreement about to be signed should be a window of opportunity.

Ruby Also, the national think tank has new research that confirms that international partnerships are great leverage for getting into new markets.

Acton That's right. So to capitalize on the opportunity, we should assign a task force to study how to best approach a partnership, what terms and agreements we want, and what incentives we can offer.

Ruby As we enter new markets, it is more important than ever to make our products intuitive, so that people across cultures find them natural to use.

Acton Our CEO always preaches about first mover advantage. So, now seems a fine time to prove good on the philosophy. We could be the first to build the next generation of products.

Ruby Well, moving abroad and moving quickly poses hazards, so we must be thoughtful, too.

Acton Plus, there might be backlash in the company if we have to downsize staff or if our products become produced too globally. We need to consider all our connections.

Ruby There's so much to consider these days! Let's just hope we turn a profit this year!

A Situation
Summarize the situation in your own words.
....
....

B Questions

1. Acton says that his company has a window of opportunity due to the new trade agreement. Have changes in the law ever created new opportunities for your company? What other **"windows of opportunity"** has your company faced? Did you try taking advantage of them? What was the result?

2. Can you think of a few reasons that **"first mover advantage"** is so good? On the other hand, while not always possible, copying a competitor's method is easier. Could you describe the costs and benefits of leading innovation?

3. Task forces are special teams designed to investigate an area or to accomplish a certain goal. Why are task forces effective? What can be their downside?

3. Language Practice

Guess the meaning of each chunk and create a new sentence.

1 window of opportunity
e.g. This year's low interest rate offered a window of opportunity to get easy credit and fund expansion.
:

2 task force
e.g. The president's task force was assigned the job to study the effect of higher tax rates on income mobility and federal revenue.
:

3 think tank
e.g. The education think tank advocated installing Wi-Fi in all classrooms and equipping each student with a tablet computer.
:

4 first mover advantage
e.g. Sometimes two companies have very similar ideas, but whoever actually produces the idea first gets first mover advantage and usually more credibility.
:

5 capitalize on
e.g. Business owners are looking for ways to capitalize on current economic conditions.
:

6 turn a profit
e.g. How soon does your company expect to turn a profit?
:

4. Role Plays

Look at each situation and role play with your partner.

A International Shipping and Logistics

A Japanese video game company is planning a product launch in the U.S. This will be the company's first entry into the U.S. market, and during the planning phase, the company discovers that its traditional ocean-based transportation and logistics model are not effective for the new market. The company must find an alternate shipping method in order to meet launch deadlines and avoid product outages on U.S. shelves. The Shipping Coordinator calls a representative for E&A Logistics, a global logistics firm, to discuss the company's needs.

Role A 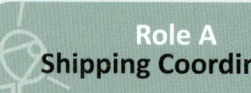 Shipping Coordinator	Role B E&A Logistics Rep.
Explains the situation and lists the company's critical requirements (e.g. a track record of on-time delivery, knowledge of both Japanese and U.S. markets, experience with a product launch, etc.)	Discusses E&A's track record, capabilities, and experience. Provides specific examples about product launches they have handled successfully.
Asks E&A to find a cost-effective, yet speedy, way to ship the video games.	Recommends chartering aircraft to transport the goods. Explains that E&A can pick up the goods from the supplier, transport them to the planes, and then offload them in the U.S.
Warns E&A that the U.S. customers have strict distribution requirements such as container sizes.	Guarantees that E&A can fulfill all of the distribution requirements, including transferring the goods from airline pallets to properly sized containers.

B. Geographical Pricing

When pricing a product, a company has to consider the costs of shipping the product to its buyer. A pricing policy may assign the shipping costs to the buyer, it may split the costs between buyer and seller, or the seller may choose to bear the entire burden. Two pricing strategies are shown below:

- **Point of Production Pricing**
  The seller quotes the selling price at the point of production and the buyer selects the method of shipping and pays the shipping costs.

- **Freight-Absorption Pricing**
  The supplier agrees to pay for some or all of the shipping costs (most often used when shipping to distant markets and such high shipping costs would put the seller at a price disadvantage to local sellers).

A construction company in Texas would like to purchase a large amount of wood from a lumber company in Oregon. The lumber company usually uses a point of production pricing strategy, but the construction company believes the shipping costs are too high and that the lumber company should absorb some of them. The Purchaser for the construction company calls the Sales Director at the lumber company.

Role A — Purchaser	Role B — Sales Director
Tells the Sales Director that they plan to order large amounts now, and in the future and that, with shipping costs, the wood is too expensive.	Tells the Purchaser that he knows a freight company that can ship the lumber at a lower cost.
Explains that the price of the lumber will still be too high.	Tells him that they can't absorb 100% of the shipping costs but that they can split it 50-50.
Explains that even at 50–50, the price will be higher than local competitors' prices.	Offers a 70-30 split and concludes the deal.

5. Business Issue & Discussion

Read the short passage and discuss the questions in as much detail as possible.

Trade Barriers vs. Free Trade

International trade reshapes the consumer landscape, offering access to a higher number and a wider variety of products. It also lowers prices of goods for which there is domestic competition and allows domestic producers the ability to ship their products abroad. With such benefits, why do so many governments hamper international trade by erecting barriers such as tariffs, quotas, and non-tariff barriers (e.g. regulating product content)?

Reasons for trade barriers include protection for domestic industries and workers, protection for consumers from unsafe products, national security, and even retaliation against another country's tariffs or foreign policy. Yet, some argue that those who are designed to benefit from trade barriers are actually being harmed.
For example, prices on goods are higher, reducing spending power, and thus destroying jobs. These critics claim that free trade is actually healthier for a country's economy and for society as a whole.

1. Discuss some other advantages and disadvantages for both trade barriers and free trade. Which do you think is best for a country and its people?
2. If you own a small, local company, which do you prefer? Why? What if you own a large, multinational company?
3. It was once said that we vote with our pocketbooks and that every purchase sends a message—for example, a consumer who does not buy domestically might be saying that the product from overseas is higher quality. If we aren't allowed to choose freely, do we lose the power to send messages?

6. Business Skills [Negotiation Skills]

Read the following short passage about "Active Listening in Negotiations" and complete the task.

Active Listening in Negotiations

A Chinese proverb states, "To listen well is as powerful a means of influence as to talk well, and is as essential to true conversation." In a negotiation, listening is just as important as talking. You must completely understand the other side's point of view and gather all of the information that you can in order to conclude a successful negotiation. But, just hearing the other person's words is not enough. A good negotiator must actively listen to his "opponent," encouraging, asking questions, repeating and summarizing, acknowledging, and empathizing.

Encouraging →	"Can you tell me more?"
Open Questioning →	"What would you like to see happen?"
Summarizing →	"Let me see if I understand what you just said."
Acknowledging →	"I can see that you feel…"
Empathizing →	"I can appreciate why you feel that way."

Task

Situation: In a negotiation, you should negotiate the sales terms for a sale/purchase of mahogany furniture from a furniture manufacturer in Indonesia to a furniture store in England. The goods will be shipped via ocean liner. It is important for both parties to consider costs, risks, and logistics during the negotiation.

1. Divide the class into two groups. With your group members, read the information about "INCOTERMS" below and talk about it.
   - **Group A:** a seller in Indonesia
   - **Group B:** a purchaser in England
2. Each group chooses a specific term among the five and discusses the reasons.
3. Both parties negotiate the sales terms and reach the final agreement.

What is "INCOTERMS"?

When negotiating an international sales contract, both parties need to pay as much attention to the terms of sale as to the sales price. Most countries have adopted an international set of trade terms (INCOTERMS), which defines the risks and responsibilities of both the buyer and seller while the goods are being shipped. The chart below summarizes the responsibilities of buyer and seller for five of the thirteen INCOTERMS. The chart also defines when the risks for the goods shift from seller to buyer.

COSTS	1 Ex Works (EXW)	2 Free On Board (FOB)	3 Cost, Insurance & Freight (CIF)	4 Delivered Duty Unpaid (DDU)	5 Delivered Duty Paid (DDP)
Warehouse Storage	Seller	Seller	Seller	Seller	Seller
Warehouse Labor	Seller	Seller	Seller	Seller	Seller
Export Packing	Seller	Seller	Seller	Seller	Seller
Loading Charges	Buyer	Seller	Seller	Seller	Seller
Inland Freight	Buyer	Seller	Seller	Seller	Seller
Terminal Charges	Buyer	Seller	Seller	Seller	Seller
Loading on Vessel	Buyer	Seller	Seller	Seller	Seller
Forwarder's Fees	Buyer	Seller	Seller	Seller	Seller
Ocean/Air Freight	Buyer	Buyer	Seller	Seller	Seller
Charges on Arrival at Destination	Buyer	Buyer	Seller	Seller	Seller
Delivery to Destination	Buyer	Buyer	Buyer	Seller	Seller
Duty, Taxes & Customs Clearance	Buyer	Buyer	Buyer	Buyer	Seller
RISKS	When the goods are at the disposal of the buyer	When the goods pass the ship's rail	When the goods pass the ship's rail	When the goods are placed at the disposal of the buyer	When the goods are placed at the disposal of the buyer

Wrapping Up!

Tell four things that you learned from this lesson to review the main ideas.

1. _____
2. _____
3. _____
4. _____

UNIT 3. Business Strategy

Lesson 12
International Markets

Learning Objectives

Upon completion of this lesson, you will be able to...
» discuss the fierce competition of markets and consumers' needs
» explain how to attract attention and promote sales

"The essence of strategy lies in creating tomorrow's competitive advantages faster than competitors can mimic the ones you possess today."
_ Gary Hamel & C. K. Prahalad

1. Warm Up Activities

A Multinational Corporations (MNCs)

Which are your favorite MNCs? Fill in the blanks with information about the companies.
Then, discuss why you like them with your partner.

No.	Company	Country	Main Service and Goods	Reasons You Like It
1.				
2.				
3.				

B Discuss the following question.

The Greek philosopher Archilochus told a fable about the Hedgehog and the Fox. In the fable, the fox knew many tricks, but the hedgehog knew only one trick. However, despite knowing only one thing, the hedgehog could defend himself against the fox. As a worker facing globalization and international competitiveness, would you rather have many skills or would you rather have one superior skill that might be better than many other skills combined?

UNIT 3. Business Strategy

Fill in the blanks with the correct words

- [ ] no-brainer
- [ ] dichotomy
- [ ] patent
- [ ] invincible
- [ ] multifaceted
- [ ] nimble
- [ ] complacent
- [ ] languish

1. too strong to be defeated : ....
2. a question or problem that is very easy to deal with : ....
3. self-satisfied but unaware or uncaring of dangers or deficiencies : ....
4. an official document that gives someone who has invented something the legal right to make or sell that invention : ....
5. a difference between two opposite things or ideas : ....
6. having many aspects; containing many features, techniques, etc. : ....
7. characterized by quick thinking, alertness, cleverness, and resourcefulness : ....
8. to become weak and unused; to become neglected : ....

2. Dialogue Practice the dialogue and answer the questions.

Smarter, not Harder

Tatiana Wow, Hunter, things have changed so much in the last ten years. Nowadays, we compete not simply with domestic competitors but firms everywhere from Copenhagen to Mumbai.

Hunter So true! On the one hand, technology and trade have boosted performance and made our products more ubiquitous. On the other hand, the advent of technology has brought us head-to-head with so many companies globally.

Tatiana Sure, technology in production, communication, and design has become swift and nimble. We can turn out a new product twice as fast as before.

Hunter Yep, using technology is surely a no-brainer, but we need to make sure that we always have new ideas on the horizon. Plus, we should always be on guard against becoming complacent.

Tatiana That's right. Not checking our weak spots could lead to big problems. Furthermore, this year's hot-seller could languish next year. So, we need to check, recheck, change, develop, and stay energized.

Hunter Also, a multifaceted attack plan guarantees that if option A fails then option B might work.

Tatiana Being globally competitive emphasizes more than ever the classic dichotomy of one core strength versus many smaller tactics.

Hunter Exactly. Sometimes, I wish that we had the perfect patent that would make us invincible. Like they say: Work smarter, not harder!

A Situation
Summarize the situation in your own words.

B Questions

1. Hunter warns against complacency, which is the mindset of assuming that things are fine how they are. Complacency is generally dangerous because things always change. How does your company guard against complacency?
2. Tatiana warns that new trends eventually become old and languish. In your industry, what changes have you noticed where what was once new has become forgotten or outdated? How do you counteract against languishing?
3. Hunter seems proud that his company's products are ubiquitous. How much do you value ubiquity? Is it always the best feature?

3. Language Practice

Guess the meaning of each chunk and create a new sentence.

1 advent of technology

e.g. With the advent of technology, society undergoes radical change.

2 head-to-head

e.g. As trade and distribution bring more companies into each other's market, head-to-head competition has become nearly unavoidable.

3 be on guard against

e.g. To keep profits up, we need to be on guard against adverse regulation as well as surprises from the competition.

4 on the horizon

e.g. To stay fresh and relevant, every season R&D puts new ideas on the horizon and eventually brings them into testing and production.

5 attack plan

e.g. As they say, sometimes the best defense is a good offense, so having an attack plan is indispensable.

6 hot-seller

e.g. The high price of gasoline will make the fuel-efficient car a hot-seller in the future.

4. Role Plays

Look at each situation and role play with your partner.

 International Branding

Farber, a baby food manufacturer, uses a picture of a smiling baby on its U.S. packaging. The company recently expanded into Africa, and its sales are extremely poor. Farber hires a marketing firm to assess the problem.
The marketing firm immediately recognizes the blunder in their international branding strategy and comes back to Farber to explain the mistake, discuss a new African strategy, and educate them about the important of branding on a country-by-country basis.

Role A Farber VP	Role B Marketing Consultant
Asks the consultant why the company's sales are so poor in Africa.	Explains that, while their brand strategy is effective in the U.S. market, it will fail in the African market. Tells him that companies usually put pictures on the label showing what is inside the package because most customers cannot read.
Expresses shock and embarrassment and asks if the company can still be successful in the African market.	Says that his marketing firm already tested the product with a new label and received positive customer feedback.
Declares that Farber will immediately redesign the African labels to include pictures of the food inside.	Highlights the importance of understanding each market and branding products specifically to the market.

B. Market Entry Strategy

A Swiss watch company, Time Tech, is currently contemplating entry into the Chinese market. Time Tech forms a new international strategy team headed by Johanna and Max to assess entry into the market. One component in the decision is the best method of entry: direct/indirect exporting, licensing, franchising, joint venture/partnership/strategic alliance, or direct investment. Johanna and Max are discussing the advantages and disadvantages of each.

Role A — Johanna	Role B — Max
Discusses indirect marketing. Points out that indirect marketing will allow faster access to the market and a less risky way to enter China, but that the company's profits will be lower and it will lose control over its Chinese sales.	Discusses licensing. Points out that the initial investment is low and allows the company to avoid trade barriers, but that again the company will give up profits to the licensee and lose control.
Suggests that the company could offer franchise opportunities, but worries that their brand is not strong enough for this type of strategy.	Discusses opening Time Tech stores in China. Points out that they will control every aspect of the business but is concerned that the investment is too large and, since this is their first global expansion, the strategy is extremely risky.
Suggests forming a joint venture with a Chinese company. Points out that the investment is fairly high and that the partner could become a competitor but that risks will be shared and it may be more effective in establishing the brand.	Agrees this may be the best strategy. Points out that it will provide a way to learn about the Chinese market and that Time Tech can combine its strengths with a Chinese partner.

5. Business Issue & Discussion

Read the short passage and discuss the questions in as much detail as possible.

Foreign Direct Investment: Positive or Negative?

As more and more companies seek to expand their operations into other countries, there is a question as to whether foreign direct investment helps or hurts a host country. Possible positive effects include:

- Encouraging growth by injecting capital into the economy.
- Generating jobs and new workplaces.
- Increasing wage levels.
- Bringing new technologies into a country.
- Creating a more highly educated and skilled workforce.
- Allowing foreign companies access to foreign markets.

However, there may also be some negative effects that offset the positives.

- Forces domestic companies to close if they cannot compete.
- Profits don't stay in the host country, but are sent back to the company's home country.
- The foreign company may use its usual suppliers, increasing imports.
- The creating of a dual economy — a developed foreign sector but underdeveloped domestic sector.
- Environmental damage and worker exploitation.

1. Do you think that foreign direct investment helps or hurts a host country?
2. Can you think of any other advantages and disadvantages to foreign direct investment?
3. How can companies wishing to invest in a foreign country avoid potentially harming the host country?

Lesson 12 / International Markets 73

6. Business Skills [Telephone Skills]

Learn some of the expressions for telephone calls and complete the task. Use the useful expressions provided while you do the task.

Understanding the International Market

A company cannot assume that a successful product in one market will be successful in another market. Each market is unique. Consumers have different needs and tastes, a brand name may not translate favorably, or the competitive environment might look completely different.

There is a seemingly endless array of factors that have to be considered when deciding to enter a foreign market.

Task

Situation: A large U.S. pizza chain is planning expansion into your home country. The company is partnering with a prominent fried chicken franchise that wants to enter the pizza market with a known U.S. brand. The pizza and chicken firms schedule a phone call to discuss the differences in the two markets.

1 Pair up and each person take one of the roles below.
- **Role A** : a representative of the U.S. pizza chain
- **Role B** : a representative of the fried chicken franchise

2 The two representatives exchange information about customer preferences/tastes, delivery methods, store size, and competition on the phone. Use the questionnaire sheet to guide your discussion.

3 Then, decide which parts of the U.S. strategy should be kept and which should be changed.

4 Note that there is a poor telephone connection as well as language difficulties complicating the phone call. Use the expression on the right.

USEFUL EXPRESSIONS

When making telephone calls, understanding the other person is sometimes challenging, especially when that person may speak a different language or there is a bad connection. If your business has international operations, partners, customers, etc., you may frequently find yourself in this situation. There are a few phrases that can be used to help the phone call run more smoothly.

- "The line is bad."
- "I think there is a problem with the connection. Let me call you right back."
- "I'm sorry. I didn't catch what you just said."
- "I didn't get that."
- "Could you repeat that, please?"
- "Could you please speak more slowly?"
- "Can you please spell that for me?"
- "Let me repeat your information to make sure I got it right."

	Questionnaire Sheet	
1.	Customer Preferences/Tastes	
2.	Competitors	
3.	Delivery Methods	
4.	Numbers and Size of the Stores	
5.	Cultural Differences	
6.		
7.		

Wrapping Up! Tell four things that you learned from this lesson to review the main ideas.

1. .... 2. .... 3. .... 4. ....

03 Out of Africa: The Egyptian Telecom's Challenge

Business Practice 2

An Egyptian company's strategy of jumping into the global market is proving that it is never too late to go global.

◉ Background

Orascom Telecom Holding (OTH) was founded by Egyptian billionaire Naguib Sawiris in 1997. Although a late starter in the telecom industry, OTH grew rapidly in emerging African markets, gaining valuable experience and accumulating profits. In 1998, it had 200,000 subscribers and now has expanded worldwide to more than 101 million subscribers.

◉ Breaking in to a Nearly Saturated Telecom Industry

OTH started as a small, Egyptian-owned company in 1997. In 2000, the company simultaneously launched into 11 different sub-Saharan African nations. By 2005, the company had sold most of its holdings (at a large profit) and began concentrating on Tunisia and Algeria. It entered post-war Iraq and later sold the network at a 350% profit. The willingness to accept large risk has created enormous profit and rocketed the company into major league status.

A Write the meanings for the following words and phrases.

- ☑ late starter: ....
- ☑ emerging markets: ....
- ☑ accumulating: ....
- ☑ expanded: ....
- ☑ launched: ....
- ☑ concentrated: ....
- ☑ major league: ....
- ☑ saturated: ....

B Talk about the following.

1. Do you think that OTH could have been so successful if it had not had the financial backing of Sawiris's billions in personal funds?
2. Sawiris took great risks but also reaped huge profits. Do you think he took these risks because he could "afford" to lose?
3. Why are telecom companies able to make such big profits even when other industries are suffering economic hardship?
4. In your country, is the telecom industry dominated by just a few companies? Who are they?
5. Do you think there is room for more companies to offer telecom services in your country or do people have enough choices now?

CASE STUDY 03

◎ The Final Frontier

OTH management strongly believes in the advantage of being first in a market. To that end, they signed a 25-year agreement to offer services in North Korea. Company executives explained that "with no competition and no licensing fees, it was a golden opportunity for OTH." Once a late-coming emerging market operator, OTH has now turned itself into a global telecoms innovator.

1. Do you think that the development of mobile services in your country has changed your country?
2. Do you think that having a mobile phone is no longer a luxury but is a necessity? Why or why not?
3. OTH has been operating in African countries and now in North Korea, where governments are dictatorial. Do you think that the company is concerned only with profit?
4. Will widespread telecom services in North Korea change the country in any way? How?

◎ Presentation

Make a presentation based on the following:

In an industry with rapidly diminishing room to accommodate late-comers, OTH grew up quickly and has elbowed its way to global prominence, where it now stands ready to shape not only the local markets in which it operates, but also the future of the telecoms industry worldwide.

Now think of a business you want to start in an emerging market and consider how you could make the business into an international enterprise. Brainstorm some of the problems you will have to face when doing business in another country based on SWOT analysis. Then, deliver your presentation.

- Emerging market (Country) : _____
- Your business (Product or service) : _____

SWOT Analysis

Strengths:	Weaknesses:
*	*
*	*
*	*

Opportunities:	Threats:
*	*
*	*
*	*

UNIT 4. Conflict Resolution

Lesson 13

Communication Breakdown

Learning Objectives

Upon completion of this lesson, you will be able to...
» define the important factors of a good communicator
» discuss how to handle a problem when communication breaks down

"I've learned that people will forget what you said, people will forget what you did, but people will never forget how you made them feel."
_ Maya Angelou

"Good communication does not mean that you have to speak in perfectly formed sentences and paragraphs. It isn't about slickness. Simple and clear go a long way."
_ John Kotter

"We have two ears and one mouth so that we can listen twice as much as we speak."
_ JEpictetus

1. Warm Up Activities

A The 7 Cs of Communication

Think of how often you communicate with people during your day. You write e-mails, have business meetings, participate in conference calls, create reports, deliver presentations, and debate with your colleagues. We spend almost our entire day communicating. According to the 7 Cs, communication needs to have the qualities listed on the right. Choose the most important one and talk with your partner.

- ☐ Clear
- ☐ Concise
- ☐ Concrete
- ☐ Correct
- ☐ Coherent
- ☐ Complete
- ☐ Courteous

B Which of the following do you think most hinders clear communication?

- ☐ **Big Ego :** Already Seems to Know the Answer
- ☐ **Lack of Trust and Respect :** Low Opinion or Lack of Harmony
- ☐ **Conflict of Interest :** Parties want opposite things, plans, directions.
- ☐ **Age/Generation Difference :** Baby-boomer, Generation X, Millenials
- ☐ **Hoarding Information :** Wants to Maintain Power
- ☐ **Hectic :** Too busy to listen well
- ☐ **Gender Difference :** Male/Female
- ☐ **Political Difference :** Conservative or Liberal

Fill in the blanks with the correct words

- ☐ concise
- ☐ viable
- ☐ candid
- ☐ ultimatum
- ☐ finite
- ☐ backfire
- ☐ productive

1. to have the opposite result to the one that was intended : ....
2. to the point; minimum; free of all superfluous detail : ....
3. making or growing things in large quantities; achieving good results : ....
4. honest and sincere; or free from bias, prejudice, or malice : ....
5. limited; determinable by counting, measurement, or thought : ....
6. capable of working, functioning, or developing : ....
7. a final demand or condition, the failure of which to achieve will cause some adverse response : ....

2. Dialogue — Practice the dialogue and answer the questions.

My Way or the Highway

Leslie Hey, it's good to catch up with you again! I'm liking all these new faces here, but sometimes I detect tension due to the generation gap.

Ryker For sure, our generation values flexibility, spontaneity, and breaking barriers. On the one hand, I certainly do not mind age, but I do insist on having people be down to earth.

Leslie Different mindsets seem to be a stumbling block to communication, but a concise set of rules could minimize that problem.

Ryker Well, have you talked to the manager lately? He's certainly down to earth, but all my recommendations fall flat with him. We really need a more viable partnership.

Leslie Indeed, he does seem to have preconceived notions about us new employees, as if all we do is Twitter and Facebook all day!

Ryker Well, we could give him some candid feedback. After all, creativity is not finite; we could innovate new practices and procedures.

Leslie Well, I just hope that if you do so that it does not backfire, with the boss giving you the famous ultimatum: My Way or the Highway!

Ryker Well, as they say, a happy worker is a productive worker. So, I might just try my luck!

A Situation
Summarize the situation in your own words.
....
....

B Questions

1. Ryker wants his co-workers to be down to earth. What do you value in a co-worker as qualities that help them listen to and understand you?

2. Leslie talks about stumbling blocks interfering with smooth communication. Has your company faced any stumbling blocks lately? How were they resolved?

3. How do you feel about ultimatums? Give a positive and a negative example of an ultimatum.

3. Language Practice

Guess the meaning of each chunk and create a new sentence.

1 generation gap

e.g. The generation gap between the baby boomers and the millennials created a bit of friction surrounded office etiquette.

:

2 stumbling block

e.g. The limited vacation time and lack of flex time proved to be a stumbling block in recruiting younger workers.

:

3 down to earth

e.g. I certainly value a cerebral thinker, but when it comes to personality and communicating the issues, being down to earth is best, I think.

:

4 fall flat

e.g. My ideas to the planning committee tend to fall flat; they never give me any positive feedback.

:

5 preconceived notions

e.g. Preconceived notions could be harmful because you assume to know every future situation based on some past example or stereotype.

:

6 try one's luck

e.g. A four-leaf clover is a token of good luck. Try your luck!

:

4. Role Plays

Look at each situation and role play with your partner.

 Crisis Communication

Crises are the ultimate unplanned events. Because of their sudden and unpredictable nature, crises strain both managers and organizations, requiring not only specialized management practices, but also unique communication strategies. Communication breakdowns during a time of crisis can permanently tarnish an organization's reputation and cause its eventual failure.

The first rule in crisis communication is to communicate, communicate, and communicate. Avoidance creates the appearance that the organization is hiding from something wrong. The organization needs to be as forthright and transparent as possible, and a response needs to come within the first few hours of the crisis.

James & James, a U.S. pharmaceutical company, has just learned that someone poisoned several bottles of its pain medication, leading to the deaths of at least five people. The Director of Corporate Communication is now speaking with a reporter in response to the developing crisis.

Role A — Reporter	Role B — Dir. of Corporate Communication
Asks for details about the problem (what happened, where did it happen, when did it happen, how did it happen, etc.)	Gives a succinct explanation of what went wrong. Expresses concern and emphasizes that public safety is the number one goal.
Asks who is to blame and what the company is doing to fix the problem.	Assures the reporter that the company is devoted to helping solve the crime. Tells the reporter that company will recall all of the medication currently on the market.
Asks what James & James will do in the future to ensure the crisis isn't repeated.	Explains that James & James is already redesigning its bottles and the medicine itself to be more resistant to tampering.

B. How Nonverbal Signals Can Affect Communication

Dr. Albert Mehrabian, a psychologist who published several works on the importance of verbal and nonverbal messages, found that when talking about feelings or attitudes, 7% of the message is conveyed through words, 38% through vocal elements (pitch, tone, rhythm, etc.), and 55% through nonverbal elements (facial expressions, gestures, posture, etc.). Consequently, communicating effectively within a business setting requires focusing equal, if not more, attention to the nonverbal portion of the exchange.

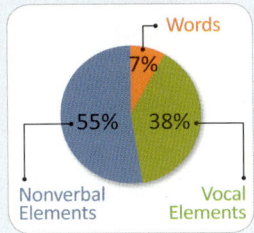

Pierre is about to tell Mark, his immediate subordinate and trusted employee for five years, about an ongoing problem. Mark has missed work a lot in the past few months and is consistently late. Pierre plans to tell Mark that his poor attendance is affecting his co-workers and the company, and that if it continues, he will have to hire someone else. At this point, Mark confesses that he was diagnosed with cancer a few months ago.
He has been receiving treatment, but sometimes feels too sick to come to work. Pierre consoles him and tries to work out a solution.

As you conduct this role play, pay close attention to the nonverbal communication that occurs. Focus on your posture, eye contact, tone, hand gestures, etc.
Are your nonverbal signals aligned with your words? Are your nonverbal signals sending conflicting messages? What are your nonverbal signals saying?

Role A — Pierre, Manager	Role B — Mark, Subordinate
Explains the problem to Mark and tells him that it is detrimental to the company.	Acknowledges the problem and its negative effects on those around him. Expresses regret for disappointing Pierre.
Warns him about similar conduct in the future.	Confesses to having cancer and explains his absences and tardiness.
Consoles Mark and asks what he can do to help. Tells Mark how much they value him and that he wants to make the situation work.	Apologizes again and tells Pierre that he doesn't want to let him down. Wants to find a solution.

Lesson 13 / Communication Breakdown

5. Business Issue & Discussion

Read the short passage and discuss the questions in as much detail as possible.

Gender and Communication Breakdown

We all know that men and women see things a bit differently. All of us can attest to that. However, scientific evidence has actually shown that men's and women's brains are not wired the same way, causing the two sexes to think in different ways and to be motivated by different things. This can cause problems not only at home, but also in the corporate setting. It is necessary to understand the tendencies of the opposite sex in order to avoid communication breakdowns and misunderstandings. While everyone is an individual and it is impossible to define hard and fast rules, there tend to be some similarities among each sex that should be considered when communicating across gender lines.

- When men use a metaphor to get a point across, they tend to use sports, whereas women prefer subjects unfamiliar to men.
- Women tend to form relationships, whereas men compete for control.
- Women are collaborative, but men are more individualistic and confrontational.
- Men like to jump in and get right to the task at hand, whereas women ask more questions and first try to understand the entire task.
- Women prefer to include and hear all the details, whereas men like to skip the details and get to the point.

1. Do you think that these gender characterizations are accurate?
2. Do you intentionally use different communication strategies with the opposite sex? Explain.
3. How could one's management styles vary based on the points above?
4. Do you think it can be dangerous to characterize employees based on sex as the article does? Can prejudging the other sex actually create miscommunication?

6. Business Skills [Feedback Skills]

Learn some of the expressions for effective feedback and complete the task.

Constructive Criticism

It has been said a million times—nobody's perfect. Everyone in an organization is going to make a mistake sooner or later. When the error is not the result of intentional negligence, it is important to help the manager or employee learn from the mistake. Constructive criticism can accomplish this, urging improvement instead of just finding faults.
When feedback is given in a positive way, it is less likely to create resentment or hurt feelings. Instead, it encourages improvement and builds trust. Here are some ways to give constructive criticism.

1. **Compliment Sandwich** → Put the bad point between two good points. "What I liked most was... One thing that could be improved is... You are so talented at..."

2. **Empathizing** → Be empathetic and express concern (this is different than pity or sympathy). "I see what you were trying to do."

3. **Leading Off Positively** → Start out by complimenting one of the person's positive characteristics. "You know, you are really good at..."

4. **Action, Not Person** → Focus on the improper action rather than a character flaw. "When you..., you did not..."

Communication Skill Activity

Materials: Sheets of paper with one geometrical pattern drawn on each sheet and blank sheets of paper.

Steps

1. Divide the class into groups and choose a leader for each group.
2. Give each group leader a sheet of paper containing a geometrical pattern. Then, give each of the group members a blank sheet of paper.
3. Position the leader with his/her back to the group so that the group members cannot see his/her face or his/her paper.
4. Without gestures, the leader must describe the pattern to the group members in a way that they can attempt to draw the pattern. (5 minutes)
5. Discuss any barriers that hindered effective communication. Practice giving constructive criticism when identifying what went wrong based on the following checklist.

Communication Skills Appraisal

	Communication Criteria	Rank (1-5)
1	**Communication Skills** ▶ The ideas are presented clearly and in a well-organized manner.	1 2 3 4 5
2	**Attention to Audience** ▶ Uses an original and creative approach for the intended audience.	1 2 3 4 5
3	**Language** ▶ Uses vivid, precise, and appropriate language. ▶ Uses good grammar to convey the message.	1 2 3 4 5
4	**Delivery** ▶ Speaks audibly, clearly, and at an effective speed. ▶ Pronunciation is easy to understand.	1 2 3 4 5
5	**Overall** ▶ Resulted in the audience understanding the message.	1 2 3 4 5

Wrapping Up!

Tell four things that you learned from this lesson to review the main ideas.

1. ....
2. ....
3. ....
4. ....

UNIT 4. Conflict Resolution

Lesson 14

Mediation & Resolution

Learning Objectives

Upon completion of this lesson, you will be able to...
» specify the different points of view and understand how to keep good relations
» know how to invite a third party's objective view

"The real art of conversation is not only to say the right thing at the right place, but to leave unsaid the wrong thing at the tempting moment."
_ Dorothy Nevill

"The horizon of many people is a circle with zero radius which they call their point of view."
_ JAlbert Einstein

"It is better to be blind than to see things from only one point of view."
_ Indian Proverb

1. Warm Up Activities

A Discuss the following questions.

A famous phrase for dealing with people and their problems is: **"Separate the person from the problem."** What does this phrase mean to you? Do you find it useful? Could you give an example of when you could or have used it?

B Employees vs. Employers

There is obviously a disconnect between employers and employees. Employers believe that monetary compensation and promotion are the main things their employees desire. However, employees want to be appreciated and cared for. What is your priority?

	What Employees Say They Want		What Employers Think Their Employees Want
1	Job security	1	Good wages
2	Full appreciation for work done	2	Job security
3	Feeling "in" on things	3	Promotion/growth opportunities
4	Sympathetic help with personal problems	4	Good working conditions
5	Good wages	5	Interesting work

UNIT 4. Conflict Resolution

Fill in the blanks with the correct words

- [ ] crisp
- [ ] composure
- [ ] endorse
- [ ] digress
- [ ] impasse
- [ ] aversion
- [ ] start up
- [ ] far-reaching

1. to turn aside from the main topic; waste time : ....
2. sharp, clean-cut, and clear : ....
3. affecting a lot of people or things in an important way : ....
4. calmness and smoothness in bearing, mind, and manners : ....
5. a deadlock; unable to go any farther in discussion or negotiation : ....
6. strong dislike and avoidance of something : ....
7. to bring a business, organization, or project into existence : ....
8. to approve openly, recommend : ....

2. Dialogue Practice the dialogue and answer the questions.

Active Listener

Ciara Working at a start-up has always been my dream! However, things here seem a little flat. We lack crisp communication.

Holt Tell me about it! Our manager seems to talk in circles about "next phase" development, but we never really get there.

Ciara On the surface, he has so much composure. Such a cool guy, I admit. However, he has a way to tilt the discussion in his favor. Plus, if you ask a direct question, he digresses off-topic, so I never hear anything quite relevant.

Holt Furthermore, he seems to have an aversion to risk and making far-reaching compromises between the different visions suggested.

Ciara True, running a company is a balancing act, but he seems a bit too self-absorbed for that.

Holt I don't mind some hierarchy as a way of managing, but in reality, workers gather around a de facto leader, the person who naturally inspires and gathers people.

Ciara Well, if he just endorsed one or two ideas coming from the bottom, I think he would win our immediate respect.

Holt That would certainly prevent any impasse in the creative process.

Ciara Reminds me of the quip: Things need management, but people need leadership.

Holt Wow! Food for thought! Somebody should write that on the letterhead!

A Situation
Summarize the situation in your own words.
....
....

B Questions

1. Holt thinks his boss talks in circles and does not address the main point. How do you feel about your boss? Is your boss a good listener?

2. Ciara likes her boss' composure, which is how he handles himself and looks on the surface. In contrast, his true management style is lacking. How much do you value composure? How much does it indicate true ability to handle people?

3. Ciara accuses her boss of "digressing," not staying on topic but drifting. Why do you think some people find it hard to stay on topic? What are some tactics to stay focused and get to the point?

4. Do you think de facto leaders are more fact or fiction? Are they more dangerous or beneficial to a company since they lead but do not have an official title?

Lesson 14 / Mediation & Resolution 83

3. Language Practice

Guess the meaning of each chunk and create a new sentence.

1 talk in circles
e.g. Once the boss starts to talk in circles, I just nod my head and pretend to agree.
:

2 tilt the discussion
e.g. To put the negotiation in your favor, you should tilt the discussion by rephrasing dialogue into more positive language and asking a few questions of your own to go on the offensive.
:

3 a balancing act
e.g. Being a parent of four children, an aspiring upper-level executive, and a night-school MBA student is such a balancing act.
:

4 de facto leader
e.g. Whereas the CEO had the title and the spacious suite, the CIO was the de facto leader because everyone listened to his advice.
:

5 make compromises
e.g. They are allowed some flexibility to negotiate and make compromises.
:

6 win respect
e.g. Winning the respect of students may seem like an arduous task for a school administrator.
:

4. Role Plays

Look at each situation and role play with your partner.

A. Managing Different Personalities

Maria was promoted to manager at her real estate firm three months ago and is now attending a two-day management seminar. This afternoon's session is centered on interpersonal skills and managing different personalities. A key point of the session is that a manager's success rests on taking the time to understand the attitudes, motivations, and tendencies of each individual employee. One of the training specialists, Marco, is discussing this with Maria.

Role A — Marco	Role B — Maria
Asks Maria about her own personality and how managers communicate with her.	Explains that she is aggressive. Her managers are direct and straightforward, but remind her who is in charge when she tries to take too much control.
Wonders if she thinks a similar management style is effective for all employees. Stresses the importance of learning about all of her employees and managing to each.	Discusses some of her employees' personalities. Asks for management tips.
Gives some suggestions about how to manage some specific personality types.	Discusses the suggestions with Marco and talks about how she will use them going forward.

01. **The Considerate** : calm; nice; thinks things through; might be slower than others and needs help making decisions.
02. **The Aggressive** : prefers taking control; makes decisions quickly
03. **The Analyst** : always sees the problems in things; plays devil's advocate
04. **The Sensitive** : feelings get hurt easily
05. **The Talkative** : shows emotion; takes a strong interest in people
06. **The Brainiac** : uses knowledge to achieve things; avoids making decisions
07. **The Quiet** : rarely speaks; seems to have low self-esteem
08. **The Results-Driven** : focuses only on achievements; loses sight of the big picture
09. **The Loner** : avoids interaction; doesn't want to be a part of the team
10. **The Overly Confident** : feels like he can do everything and is never wrong
11. **The Curmudgeon** : grumpy; pessimistic; doesn't like supervision
12. **The Mean-Spirited** : complains about everything

B. Labor Unions and Strikes

The Atlanta public school system is facing a crisis. Following a series of violent crimes, the Atlanta Teacher's Union demanded that metal detectors be installed in schools citywide. The School Superintendent believed that metal detectors were too costly and wouldn't reduce school violence. Instead, he put extra security guards in the schools. However, the union still says it is not enough and is currently threatening to go on strike. The Superintendant wants to avoid a strike and is sitting down with a union representative to discuss their different points of view.

 Role A Union Representative	 Role B School Superintendant
Reiterates the union's demands. Explains why metal detectors are necessary and why extra security guards don't provide enough protection.	Tells the union rep that metal detectors are too costly and will result in lower pay and other major budget cuts.
Threatens a strike unless the Superintendant meets their demands.	Points out the negative effects of striking. Warns the union rep that he could replace the striking teachers permanently. Asks for a compromise.
Informs the Superintendant that the union would be willing to accept equipping security guards with less expensive metal detector wands.	Feels that this option is much more reasonable and that he can accommodate the union. Thanks the union rep for coming to an agreement.

5. Business Issue & Discussion

Read the short passage and discuss the questions in as much detail as possible.

Teams: Love Them or Hate Them

Someone once said, "A job worth doing is worth doing together." While managers would support this opinion, regarding teamwork as a key driver of success within an organization, it turns out that employees might not view teamwork so favorably. One study on the perception of teamwork showed that 75% of employees prefer to work on their own. Yet another study showed that 40% of employees agree with the statement, "If you want something done right, you have to do it yourself." Of the employees surveyed, 16% said they go as far as declining to work in teams. If this is the case, management truly has their work cut out for them. How can a manager expect his or her team to stimulate creativity, accomplish tasks more quickly, or bring employees closer together if the team members don't even want to be there in the first place?

1. Do you feel that there are situations in which working alone is more beneficial? Why do you feel this way? Do you think teamwork is important in an organization?
2. Why do you think a majority of employees prefer to work independently?
3. How can managers change employees' attitudes about teams?

6. Business Skills [Communication Skills in Mediation]

Read the following short passage about "Productive Mediation". Then, choose a situation among three and complete the task as a group work.

The Mediator Hat

Managers wear many hats, and one of them is the mediator hat. Often, disputes arise between two parties (two co-workers, a manager and subordinate, etc.) and the manager is stuck in the middle to play referee. Below is a set of tips that will help keep the mediation focused and productive and lead to resolving the conflict.

TIP 01 Pay Attention
Give the speaker your full attention. You posture should do the same. Make eye contact and don't cross your arms, play with papers, or make faces.

TIP 02 Paraphrase and Summarize
Restate or summarize what the speaker has said in your own words.
▸ "What I hear you saying is…"
▸ "What I understand you both to be saying is…"
▸ "So you feel angry about…"

TIP 03 Ask Clarifying Questions
Ask open-ended questions to obtain more information or to clarify the speaker's view.
▸ "Tell me more about…"
▸ "Can you give an example of…?"

TIP 04 Focus on the Problem, Not the Person
Don't assign blame or find fault. Instead, focus on the issues at hand.

TIP 05 Speak from Your Own Perspective
Describe your own thoughts, feelings, and values.
▸ "I feel…/ I believe… / I think…"

TIP 06 Speak Directly to the Other Person
▸ "What do you want to do about this…?"

TIP 07 Be Specific
Avoid using "always" and "never." Give concrete examples.

TIP 08 Build for the Future
Don't argue about the past. Talk about how things should be in the future.

TIP 09 Focus on Common Interests, Not Positions
A position is often a demand, whereas an interest is an underlying value, concern, need, or fear. While two parties positions may be opposite to each other, their interests may not be.

TIP 10 Create Options for Mutual Gain
Try to find solutions that benefit both parties' interests.

TIP 11 Foster an Atmosphere of Cooperation and Collaboration

Task

1. Get into groups of three. Choose two of the group members to dispute one of the following topics.
2. The third group member will mediate, using the steps above to resolve the conflict.
3. After the mediation is finished, the two disputers assess their mediation experience. Then, discuss what may have gone wrong, how the mediation could have been better, and what you learned from it.

Situation 1 A salesman feels that one of his fellow salesmen is contacting his long-time clients, taking them out to dinner and buying them drinks in an attempt to "steal" them so that he can increase his sales commission. The other salesman believes that the company policies don't prohibit this and that he is not doing anything wrong.

Situation 2 A female employee feels that her manager is purposely giving her poor evaluations because she often has to go home early to take care of her children. She feels that she has actually accomplished more than her male team members but that the manager, who is also a male, is just playing favorites with the males. The manager claims that her poor performance reviews are because she refuses to cooperate on projects and isn't a team player.

Situation 3 An employee feels that the lighting in the office is not adequate and causing her health problems. He has informed his manager of the situation, but nothing has been changed. The manager claims that nobody else in the office has a problem and that changing the lighting is a waste of money.

Wrapping Up! Tell four things that you learned from this lesson to review the main ideas.

1. _____ 2. _____ 3. _____ 4. _____

UNIT 4. Conflict Resolution

Lesson 15

Cross-cultural Differences

Learning Objectives

Upon completion of this lesson, you will be able to...
» specify the cultural differences and barriers to communication
» become more aware of cultural etiquette and become more open-minded

"We become not a melting pot but a beautiful mosaic. Different people, different beliefs, different yearnings, different hopes, different dreams."
_ Jimmy Carter

"Each of us shines in a different way, but this doesn't make our light less bright."
_ Albert Einstein

1. Warm Up Activities

A Discuss the following questions.

Q1. Have you ever had any problems with co-workers due to cultural difference?
If not personally, have you ever seen such problems in media such as film, books, news?

Q2. Why is cultural understanding important in business? Give specific examples.

Q3. What do you do to improve your cross-cultural competence?

Q4. When you go abroad, what do you miss most about your own culture?

B Is that Culture?

Here is a list of behaviors. In the blanks, put a "U" if you think the behavior is universal, "C" if it is cultural, or "P" if it is personal.

1. Considering pigs to be "good luck". .... [   ]
2. Sleeping with a bedroom window half-open. .... [   ]
3. Running from a dangerous animal. .... [   ]
4. Men opening doors for women. .... [   ]
5. Preferring reading a book to playing baseball. .... [   ]
6. Feeling sad at the death of your mother. .... [   ]
7. Respecting older people. .... [   ]
8. Calling a waiter with a hissing sound. .... [   ]

Answers: 1-C, 2-P, 3-U, 4-C, 5-P, 6-U, 7-C, 8-C

Lesson 15 / Cross-cultural Differences

Fill in the blanks with the correct words

☐ localization
☐ assimilate
☐ embrace
☐ inclusion
☐ convey
☐ impediment
☐ hostile

1. to accept readily; include as a part of a larger whole : ....
2. to impart or communicate verbally or by gesture or indication : ....
3. showing unfriendly feeling or outright opposition : ....
4. Setting up a branch, office, or operations in another country and adapting to the market and way of life there : ....
5. acceptance into the greater group : ....
6. a blockage or something that interferes : ....
7. to take on and fit into the surrounding or dominant culture into which a person has moved : ....

2. Dialogue   Practice the dialogue and answer the questions.

Cultural Intelligence

Ayla Having such a diverse workforce is surely an asset, but sometimes all sorts of impediments prevent us from seeing eye-to-eye.

Royce For sure! I have tried small talk as way to build a tie, but sometimes I crave major tactics to convey deep cultural insights.

Ayla Unfortunately, I don't think that you and I can take a crash course. We'll just have to assimilate over time even though speed is the essence of most business these days.

Royce Sometimes cultural cues are even more important than the message itself in order to be understood and accepted.

Ayla Right on. We need to practice true localization. We can't just be here, but we truly have to be a part of the social fabric to create acceptance and avoid misunderstanding.

Royce It's funny: sometimes products are attractive and embraced because of their "foreignness," and other times they are rejected for that very reason.

Ayla Exactly, it is hard to know in advance when your product will miss the mark in the foreign market.

Royce So far, no one has been openly hostile, but we shouldn't mistake that for total inclusion either.

Ayla Now I see why "cultural intelligence" is listed as a necessary aptitude in the modern CEO.

A Situation
Summarize the situation in your own words.

....
....

B Questions

1. Royce mentions how **"foreignness"** can be both an attraction and repulsion regarding both products and people. Do you agree or disagree? Why do you think humans show this trait?

2. Ayla talks about true **"localization,"** which means getting an outside company to fit almost naturally to the foreign market. How important is "localization" to foreign success? Isn't success mostly dependent on superior products, pricing, and distribution?

3. Ayla mentions taking a cash course. The crash course would be for **"assimilation,"** getting to know and adapting to the new country in which she and Royce live. When workers go to a different country, who is most responsible for encouraging assimilation: the corporation, the native government, or the individual?

3. Language Practice

Guess the meaning of each chunk and create a new sentence.

1 see eye-to-eye
e.g. Seeing eye-to-eye is critical to keeping a smooth work relationship.
:

2 crash course
e.g. Since his boss announced the Tokyo trip with less than two weeks to get ready, Franklin decided to take a crash course in Japanese.
:

3 cultural cue
e.g. Not smiling is not necessarily a negative cultural cue in some countries; in fact, it could be positive.
:

4 social fabric
e.g. By taking part in the language club and attending the new volunteer committee, Lynn hoped to be more of a part of the social fabric.
:

5 miss the mark
e.g. By stressing cheapness in a culture that values luxury, we totally missed the mark.
:

6 small talk
e.g. Whether you are holding the meeting or attending the meeting, it is polite to make small talk while you wait for the meeting to start.
:

4. Role Plays

Look at each situation and role play with your partner.

A. Body Language in Different Cultures

The best thing that you can do before interacting with someone from another country is to study the culture and learn the customs. However, expecting to know everything about the other culture is unreasonable. Trying to remain perfect will add to your anxiety and cause you to act unnaturally. Sooner or later, you will commit a cultural blunder that causes the other individual discomfort.

When this occurs, it is important to apologize and recover from the mistake so that the business relationship is not permanently damaged.

TIP.
1. Apologize and express regret about the offensive words or actions.
2. Don't try to justify the error. It will probably cause more problems.
3. Express a desire to respect the person and the culture.
4. Use it as a learning experience. Convey a willingness to find out more about the culture. Ask what you did wrong and how it can be corrected.
5. Don't repeat the mistake.
6. Move on.

Choose one of the following cultural blunders to role play.

1. A U.S. businessman is meeting with a Saudi Arabian counterpart. During the meeting, he crosses his ankle over his leg and exposes the bottom of his shoe, oblivious to his offense.
2. A British businesswoman is meeting with a Brazilian businessman. The British woman gives the "OK" symbol with her hand, not knowing that it is a serious insult.
3. A Japanese company is hosting a dinner for an Australian client. While eating, one of the Australians sticks his chopsticks upright in his bowl of rice, unaware that it is a funeral ritual.

Role A The Offender	Role B The Offended
Makes a cultural mistake.	Acts offended and informs the offender of his error.
Apologizes for the mistake using the six steps above.	Listens to the offender's apology and helps to move on.

B Language Barriers

Three years ago, a Canadian company opened a sales office in Argentina. All of the company's research indicated that the Argentineans would love its products, but sales figures are still very poor. The Sales Manager in Argentina analyzed the situation and found that the Argentinean customers were hesitant to do business with an all-Canadian sales force that spoke only English. They believed that the company was not interested in making long-term relationships and could not be trusted. The Sales Manager in Argentina calls the Vice President at the head office with the news.

Role A	Sales Manager, Argentina	Role B	Vice President
Tells the Vice President about the problems that the language barrier is creating.		Expresses surprise and disappointment that the sales force still hasn't learned any.	
Suggests hiring a few translators and native Argentinean sales representatives.		Agrees with the suggestion. Demands language courses so that the Canadians can learn some key words and polite phrases.	
Says that he will enroll his sales force in language courses right away and apologizes repeatedly.		Informs him that he will monitor the progress of the Argentinean office.	

5. Business Issue & Discussion

Read the short passage and discuss the questions in as much detail as possible.

Cultural Differences and Stereotyping

One of the most famous works in the field of cultural differences came from Geerte Hofstede in 1980. Hofstede proposed that five dimensions could be used to define a country's culture (shown below). Each country would then receive a score for each dimension so that countries could be compared against each other (also shown below). For example, an individualistic society places more importance on self and receives a higher score, whereas a collective society emphasizes the group and receives a lower score.

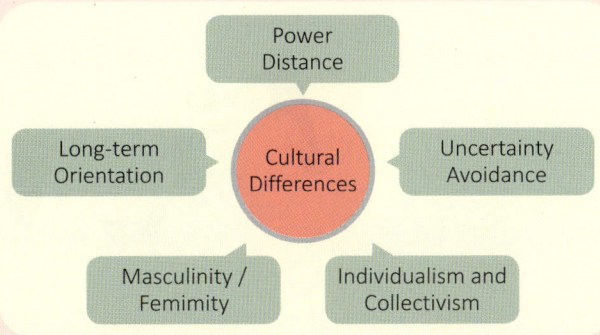
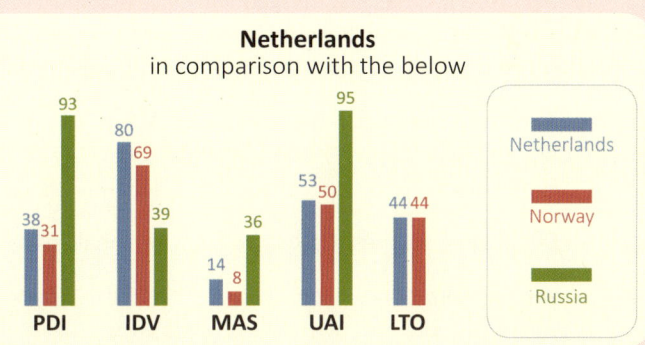

However, critics have claimed that Hofstede's research has propagated stereotyping—making general assumptions about—cultures. The scores of a country are averages and do not speak to individual characteristics. It is dangerous to assume that everyone within the country will fit into a defined cultural group. While Hofstede warned about the dangers of stereotyping, managers who use these types of cultural models risk the potential to stereotype.

1. Do you think research like Hofstede's is useful when managing people from different cultures?
2. Does Hofstede's research lead to stereotypes? What types of stereotypes do you have about certain cultures, and how would that affect your communication style?
3. How do you think your culture fits into the model? Would it accurately define you?

6. Business Skills [Presentation Skills]

Learn some of the expressions for business presentation and complete the task.

Training Others

At some point during your professional career, you will most likely have to train others, whether it is a new employee or an entire sales force. In order for your presentation to be successful, it will need to be effective, engaging, and easy to follow. Signpost language guides the listener through the presentation and tells the listener what has just happened and what is going to happen next.

1. Introducing the Topic →	▸ "My topic today is…" ▸ "My talk is concerned with…"
2. Overview →	▸ "There are a number of points I'd like to make…" ▸ "During my presentation, I will cover…"
3. Finishing a Section / Starting a New Section →	▸ "We've looked at…" ▸ "Moving on now to…"
4. Analyzing a Point →	▸ "Let's consider this in more detail…" ▸ "What does this mean for…?" ▸ "The significance of this is…"
5. Giving Examples →	▸ "A good example of this is…" ▸ "To illustrate this point…"
6. Summarizing and Concluding →	▸ "Unfortunately, I seem to have run out of time, so I'll conclude very briefly by saying that…" ▸ "In short…"

Task

Situation: ABC Inc. has just merged with XYZ Inc. The two organizations are located in different countries. As the Human Resources Manager for XYZ Inc., it is your responsibility to deliver a presentation to the employees of ABC Inc. about the cultural norms in XYZ's home country.

1 Choose three things which the employees of ABC Inc. should be well aware of.

- ☐ Eye Contact
- ☐ Handshakes
- ☐ Greetings
- ☐ Exchanging Business Cards
- ☐ Personal Space
- ☐ Touching
- ☐ Personal Dress / Hygiene
- ☐ (Hand) Gestures
- ☐ Table Manners
- ☐ Tipping

2 Think about several examples of the cultural norms you chose. In order to keep your presentation interesting, make sure to involve the audience with a demonstration, game, or activity.

3 Make a presentation based on what you prepared. Use the presentation expressions to make it effective.

Wrapping Up!
Tell four things that you learned from this lesson to review the main ideas.

1. _____   2. _____   3. _____   4. _____

UNIT 4. Conflict Resolution

Lesson 16
Business Ethics

Learning Objectives

Upon completion of this lesson, you will be able to...
» exchange opinions about business ethics and morals
» discuss real cases related to ethics and indicate the right and wrong

> "Try not to become a man of success,
> but rather try to become a man of value."
> _ Albert Einstein

> "History shows that where ethics and conomics
> come in conflict, victory is always with economics.
> Vested interests have never been known to have willingly divested
> themselves unless there was sufficient force to compel them."
> _ B. R. Ambedkar

1. Warm Up Activities

A Which of the following two would most bother you? Why?

- ☐ **An investment banker** lied about how much money you could make or the quality of an investment.
- ☐ **An auto-repairman** lied about needing to fix something that was not actually broken.
- ☐ **The president** manipulated the jobs report to make the economy look stronger than reality so that he could get re-elected.
- ☐ **An art dealer** forged the signature on an otherwise magnificent painting to make it appear as if done by a famous painter.
- ☐ **An hourly employee** counts as work hours time spent on Facebook or on personal activities.
- ☐ **On a business trip, a worker** uses the company account to pay for personal items or spends a bit extravagantly.
- ☐ **Employees** use the company printer to print personal items.
- ☐ **Your doctor** wrote prescribe medicine which you did not necessarily need.
- ☐ **A taxi driver** drove a longer route on purpose.

B Discuss the following questions.

Q1. What do you think is the purpose of a business? Is it just to make money?
Q2. What do you understand by the term "an ethical business"?

Fill in the blanks with the correct words

- ☐ subtlety
- ☐ resist
- ☐ norms
- ☐ falsify
- ☐ fraudulent
- ☐ interplay
- ☐ condemn
- ☐ preach

1. to express a strong opinion and try to persuade other people to accept it : ....
2. to exert force in opposition : ....
3. something that is difficult to interpret; small detail : ....
4. the ways that people or things affect each other or react when they are put together : ....
5. to change something deliberately in order to trick people : ....
6. characterized by fraud or deceit; false, fake : ....
7. normal, customary, or regular behavior; customs : ....
8. to declare against something as evil, wrong, or reprehensible : ....

2. Dialogue   Practice the dialogue and answer the questions.

Fudging the Numbers

Jacintha Really, it's quite shocking to hear the news. Braxton seemed to be full of so much moral fiber.

Langston Yes, it seems that he just could not resist being fraudulent on that earning's report. He's been fudging the numbers for quite awhile now, it appears.

Jacintha Makes you wonder what else might turn up! Really, we should try to rein in any chance for falsification. Maybe an automatic alert system could screen for irregularity.

Langston Sure, it would be a smart defense if the computer system could raise a red flag for any suspicious activity.

Jacintha Well, to be fair and not condemn him outright, some of his work dealt with the subtlety between right and wrong.

Langston I admit it sure was a gray area at times. However, he knows the company norms. In fact, he preached them more than anybody.

Jacintha Too true! Sometimes wrong choices happen due to the interplay of temptation, gain, and rationalization. So, I don't judge too harshly, but there should be a way out.

Langston Really, this whole incident just reminds us that we need to work harder to make a moral compass part of the company mission.

A Situation
Summarize the situation in your own words.

....
....

B Questions

1. Jacintha talks about Braxton's lack of moral fiber, which is the moral quality of a person. How would you define your moral fiber? Can you give an example from your work life or how you treat customers?

2. A **"gray area"** is a way to explain a situation where right and wrong (black and white) mix so that it is hard to know what is perfectly legal or right. Can you give an example of gray areas? How do you deal with gray areas?

3. Fudging numbers is lying about data; it could be big, or it could be small. How much of a danger do you see **"fudging the numbers"** to be to a company?

4. Langston talks about the development of a strong **"moral compass"** being a part of the solution.
A moral compass is a person's "inner sense of right and wrong," like a personal conscience when nobody is looking. How much do you think that success depends on a strong moral compass? Can you explain the cause and effect?

3. Language Practice

Guess the meaning of each chunk and create a new sentence.

1 fudge the number

e.g. Unemployment was up last year, but the Labor Bureau had been fudging the numbers.
:

2 rein in

e.g. To balance the budget, Congress needs to rein in reckless spending.
:

3 moral fiber

e.g. The board of directors would like to make testing for moral fiber a part of the hiring and promotion process.
:

4 raise a red flag

e.g. The number of law grads who cannot even get a job should raise a red flag that most law schools are overpriced.
:

5 moral compass

e.g. A good test of your moral compass is what you do when faced with temptation when nobody is looking and probably cannot find out about what you did.
:

6 screen for

e.g. We monitor building entrances to screen for people not meeting a client's profile.
:

7 gray area

e.g. At the moment, the law on compensation is a gray area.
:

4. Role Plays

Look at each situation and role play with your partner.

A. Unethical Behavior Forced Upon You

If a manager paints you into an ethical corner by requesting that you do something immoral, how would you respond? Would you go along with it and hope not to get caught? Would you stand up to your boss even if it resulted in negative consequences? Does it depend on the severity of the request? Does size even matter in ethics, or is wrong always wrong?

Greg is a junior architect at a Boston architecture firm. He and the firm were just awarded a contract to design the city's new art museum. Anytime that he works on the project, he must document the hours and create billing invoices for the company's client, the city of Boston. But, whenever Bill submits his invoices for review, his manager requests that he increase the hours so that the firm can charge the city more money. His manager explains that this is a common practice, that the city can afford to pay for the extra hours, that the firm deserves the extra money, and that he hopes Greg is a team player. Greg complies the first few times, but doesn't feel comfortable with the situation anymore. He approaches his manager.

Role A — Greg	Role B — Greg's Manager
Informs his manager of his personal moral dilemma and that he can no longer sign the falsified invoices.	Assures Greg that he isn't doing anything morally wrong, just "fudging" the numbers. Tells Greg that he is new to the business and doesn't understand how things really work.
Refrains from criticizing his manager, but says that it's not something he wants to do for personal reasons. Asks his manager to sign the invoices instead of him.	Declines to sign the invoices for Greg. Tells Greg that he needs to think about the company and that Greg isn't being a team player. Asks Greg to reconsider.
Reiterates his position and gives the opinion that it isn't in the best interest of the company. Suggests speaking to upper level management about it.	Refuses to talk to upper level management. Accepts the invoices as-is but suggests that Greg think about his future.

UNIT 4. Conflict Resolution

B. Discrimination and Promotion

Nicole, an Australian citizen who is bilingual in Thai and English, has lived and worked in Thailand for over ten years. She has been one of the top salespeople at her company, a Thai beverage company, for the past seven years, but has seen numerous local Thais promoted to sales managers ahead of her. She was recently passed over for another promotion, and when she talked to her manager about it, he claimed that someone else was more qualified than she was. Nicole feels that she is being discriminated against because she is a woman and because she is a foreigner. She requests a meeting with Isra in HR to discuss it.

Role A — Nicole	Role B — Isra
Claims that the company is discriminating against her. Gives a short summary of the situation.	Asks if she has talked to her manager about it and suggests that maybe the others were more qualified.
Tells her that she has talked to the manager many times, but the manager never gives her specific reasons for the promotion choice. Informs her that her sales record is well-documented with stellar performance reviews and client testimonials.	Asks if she has expressed her desire to be moved in the manager role.
Says that she has told her manager about her career goals on several occasions. Reiterates her past accomplishments and loyalty to the company.	Tells her that she will look into the situation and that if discrimination has occurred it will be corrected.

5. Business Issue & Discussion

Read the short passage and discuss the questions in as much detail as possible.

Corporate Social Responsibility

Corporate social responsibility (CSR), or the activities that an organization takes to integrate economic, social, and environmental concerns into its business, is a relatively new term, but not a new concept. In fact, examples of socially and environmentally conscious corporate practices can be traced back thousands of years. However, whereas companies of the past could have ignored concerns other than profits, it seems that CSR is now a necessary component of business strategy. Examples of CSR are everywhere—from the cosmetics company that claims to abstain from testing on animals to a beer company that invests in responsible drinking education to a food processing company that contributes to hunger relief in Africa. But, what are the motives behind CSR?

A study that surveyed Dutch managers about CSR found that some saw it as their moral duty to exhibit socially responsible behavior, motivated not by money but by altruism. Is this to be believed? If their companies' profits decreased as a result of CSR, would it continue?

In truth, CSR is nothing more than an advertising scheme. Companies that engage in CSR do so to advertise their behavior, differentiate their products, increase profits, and boost market share. In this sense, CSR is one big marketing decision. For example, if CSR were really an altruistic action then gas companies would offer more eco-friendly fuel. Because consumers will not pay more for the "green" fuel, the gas companies will not sacrifice profits for environmental responsibility. So, let's label CSR for what it is—not doing good to do good, but doing good to improve the bottom line.

1. Do you agree that CSR is just another way for companies to increase their profits?
2. If you were a manager, would you engage in CSR if it weren't profitable?
3. Can you think of some real world examples of CSR? Are any of them altruistic, or do they all contribute to the bottom line in some form or another?

6. Business Skills [Meeting Skills]

Learn some of the expressions for business meeting and complete the task.

Chairing a Meeting

Most meetings require a chairperson in order to control and direct the proceedings. An effective chairperson keeps the course of the meeting in line with the agenda, and a meeting without a chairperson is like an orchestra without a conductor—a lot of noise, but no real harmony. While the participants in the meeting are the major drivers of success, a chairperson plays a critical role in starting the meeting, setting the agenda, keeping the participants' eyes on the meeting objectives, moving them from one topic to another, and bringing the meeting to a close.

1. Welcoming	4. Moving to the First Item
▸ "I want to thank everyone for coming." ▸ "Well, a warm welcome to everyone here."	▸ "Why don't we begin with...?" ▸ "The first thing we need to consider is..."

2. Starting the Discussion	5. Checking for Final Comments
▸ "Let's get down to business." ▸ "The purpose of this meeting is..."	▸ "Does anyone have anything else?" ▸ "Would anyone like to make any further comments?"

3. Stating the Objectives	6. Closing
▸ "We're here today to..." ▸ "The purpose of this meeting is..."	▸ "If there's nothing else, let's wrap up." ▸ "Okay, let's call it a day. Thanks everyone."

Task

1. Read three situations (Situation 01-03) presented below.
2. Use the three-step checklist below to determine whether or not the actions demonstrate ethical behavior.
3. Once you have finished your assessments, get into groups of three. Take turns chairing meetings that address the morality of the situations.

Situation 01
YM Motors is a large automobile manufacturer. Its safety division recently found a way to cut costs by using less expensive materials in its seatbelts. However, the change will cause failure rates to increase from 0.12% to 0.15%. Nevertheless, the failure rate of 0.15% still falls below the government standard of 0.20%.

Situation 02
Christina is a customer service representative at a major credit card company. She has access to the entire database and can view customers' confidential information. She sometimes looks up the records of celebrities, entertainers, and politicians to see where they spend their money and how much they spend. She then tells her friends about it.

Situation 03
Henry is a waiter at an upscale steak restaurant. He recently overheard two of his customers discussing an upcoming merger between two major electronics firms. Knowing that, Henry bought stock in the companies and profited enormously when the merger occurred.

THREE STEP CHECKLIST

1. Is the action illegal? Explain your reasoning.

2. Does the action violate professional standards?

3. Who is affected and how?

People Affected	
Negative Effects	
Positive Effects	

Wrapping Up!

Tell four things that you learned from this lesson to review the main ideas.

1. _____ 2. _____ 3. _____ 4. _____

04 McDonald's Conquers the Land of Haute Cuisine

How McDonald's entered the French market successfully, struggling through social and cultural controversy with sound resolutions.

◉ Background

The foray into France was a rocky road for McDonald's. In 1999, political activists bulldozed a McDonald's store into the ground. With many changes and a focused effort to appease cultural tastes, the chain has grown to more than 1,200 restaurants throughout the country at a rate of 30 new franchises a year.

◉ Recognizing differences

McDonald's was unprepared for the reaction of the French when it moved its American-style fast food burger into the country. Overall, the chain was not responding to local market needs and opportunities. They were trying to offer "a slice of America" in France. But in France, barely 10% of meals are eaten outside the home, compared to nearly 40% in the US. Adapting to a completely new (and sometimes hostile) market was a challenge.

1 What kinds of things might McDonald's need to know about French culture?

✓		Very Important	Moderately Important	Not Important
01	French people don't snack between meals.			
02	French people take a long time for their meals.			
03	French people eat more sandwiches than burgers.			
04	French people consider themselves intellectuals.			
05	The trend in France is for healthy eating.			
06	French fries originated in Belgium.			
07	Roman Catholic is the dominant religion.			
08	Wine is served at most meals.			
09	French take great pride in their cuisine.			
10	French society is very class distinctive.			
11	Paris is the no. 1 tourist destination in the world.			
12	Burger King failed when trying to enter the French market.			
13	Each region of France has its own cuisine.			

2 Talk about the following questions.

a. Why do you think McDonald's had so many difficulties breaking into the French market?

b. McDonald's has had success by offering the same food in all its stores. Why do you think this was a problem in France?

c. What is your opinion of McDonald's food?

d. Has McDonalds been successful in your country? Why (or why not) have they been successful?

e. Do you think owning a McDonald's franchise would give you a successful business in your country?

CASE STUDY 04

◎ Analyzing the Success Factors

McDonald's was able to overcome the initial resistance of the French and is finally thriving. The three main reasons for McDonald's success are the following:

» Local responsiveness (changing the menu),
» Rebranding (changing décor and offering table service), and
» A robust corporate ecosystem (purchasing all ingredients locally and recycling as much as possible).

The changes were initiated by members of local management, who have autonomy from the American Head Office in decision-making on these issues. Discuss the five questions and analyze the success factors.

1. Considering all the changes that were made to make McDonald's "accepted" in France, do you think the chain has lost its identity (compromised its worldwide branding)?
2. Do you think the success in France will serve as a model for McDonald's to expand into other countries that could also be culturally sensitive?
3. McDonald's food has often been referred to as "junk food." What is junk food and why is McDonald's labeled as such?
4. What are your personal preferences when going out to eat? What are the important factors when considering a restaurant?
5. Has McDonald's made changes to its menu in your country? What are some of the items served in your country that would not be found in the US?

◎ Presentation

Make a presentation based on the following:
You should prepare a list of cultural issues that must be considered before opening a restaurant franchise business in a foreign country. How would you market your restaurant? What factors must you consider about cultural tastes before opening your restaurant? How would you alter your menu (or not) to be successful in the country's market?

1. In which country are you going to open the restaurant? (e.g., China) ....
2. Make a list of considerations which you should think of before opening the restaurant.

*	*
*	*
*	*

ANSWER KEY — Business Practice 2

Unit 1. Self Management

Lesson 01
Career & Success

① assessment
② fringe benefits
③ micromanage
④ meticulous
⑤ autonomous
⑥ golden handshake
⑦ expedite
⑧ delegate

Lesson 02
Time Management

① prioritize
② persistent
③ punctual
④ procrastinate
⑤ tardy
⑥ contingency
⑦ consolidate
⑧ constraint

Lesson 03
Leadership & Management Style

① charisma
② gutsy
③ shrewd
④ empathy
⑤ morale
⑥ polarizing
⑦ audacious

Lesson 04
Stress Management

① momentum
② downtime
③ burnout/ burned out
④ fatigue
⑤ barrier
⑥ clutter
⑦ trade-off

Unit 2. Project Management

Lesson 05
Budgeting

① benchmark
② inertia
③ frugal
④ forecast
⑤ panacea
⑥ leverage
⑦ dearth
⑧ tight-fisted

Lesson 06
Production Management

① emulate
② hobbled
③ megatrend
④ unveil
⑤ volatile
⑥ resilience
⑦ game-changer

Lesson 07
Monitoring & Feedback

① empathy
② tackle
③ exude
④ forthright
⑤ buzzword
⑥ gravitas
⑦ pitfall

Lesson 08
Risk Management

① catastrophe
② fallout
③ agile
④ aftermath
⑤ toxic
⑥ avert
⑦ dilemma
⑧ foreseeable
⑨ paralysis

Unit 3. Business Strategy

Lesson 09
Strategic Planning
① obsolete
② formulate
③ murky
④ savvy
⑤ downside
⑥ infringe
⑦ pre-emptive

Lesson 10
Strategic Analysis
① template
② prediction
③ hone
④ modify
⑤ out-of-touch
⑥ simulate
⑦ validate
⑧ crucial

Lesson 11
International Commerce
① backlash
② enhance
③ hazard
④ downsize
⑤ turbulence
⑥ intuitive
⑦ sluggish

Lesson 12
International Markets
① invincible
② no-brainer
③ complacent
④ patent
⑤ dichotomy
⑥ multifaceted
⑦ nimble
⑧ languish

Unit 4. Conflict Resolution

Lesson 13
Communication Breakdown
① backfire
② concise
③ productive
④ candid
⑤ finite
⑥ viable
⑦ ultimatum

Lesson 14
Mediation & Resolution
① digress
② crisp
③ far-reaching
④ composure
⑤ impasse
⑥ aversion
⑦ start up
⑧ endorse

Lesson 15
Cross-cultural Differences
① embrace
② convey
③ hostile
④ localization
⑤ inclusion
⑥ impediment
⑦ assimilate

Lesson 16
Business Ethics
① preach
② resist
③ subtlety
④ interplay
⑤ falsify
⑥ fraudulent
⑦ norms
⑧ condemn

BUSINESS PRACTICE

2

BUSINESS PRACTICE Series
Focuses on various situations involved in business while providing opportunities to improve learners' communication skills in the workplace.

CARROT HOUSE

CARROT HOUSE
P.O.Box #2924, St. Marys, Ontario, Canada

Business Practice 2
© Carrot House

All rights reserved. No part of this publication may be reproduced, stored in a retrieval system, or transmitted in any form or by any means without the prior permission in writing of Carrot House

First Printed April 2014

Author: Carrot Language Research & Development, Canada
Acquisitions Editor: Edita Co., US

ISBN 978-89-6732-117-8

Printed and distributed in Korea
9th Fl., Daenam Building, 199, Nonhyeon-dong
Gangnam-gu, Seoul, South Korea 135-827